"This book is fantastic
every HR person every
that you can almost imagine the scenarios, but at the same
time grasp the implications of what is being explained and
how to navigate a process that may be daunting to all
involved. This book makes it less daunting and feels like
Kelly's voice is in your ear throughout.

Since 2014, Kelly has provided legal and HR advice to our
company. I have constantly been impressed by her
professionalism, her practical approach and her ability to see
the big picture for her clients. Her knowledge and
experience go without saying but on top of that she can
explain legal terminology and requirements in such a way
that it is easy to understand the logic and the process."

SHEREE LYNCH, Director,
Operations, MHG Insurance Brokers

"As an attorney who has practiced employee-side
employment law for 31 years, it is refreshing to see a book
dedicated to real, effective workplace investigations.
Attorney Charles-Collins dives straight into the messy
world of investigating employee complaints, and explains
why employers should take them seriously and not retaliate.
Too many employers immediately go into self-protection
mode when they receive a complaint and try to discredit the
victim instead of conducting a serious investigation to get to
the truth. If employers follow the easy step-by-step process
Attorney Charles-Collins lays out, they can improve
workplace morale and avoid the disastrous publicity of a
#MeToo situation."

DONNA BALLMAN,
Employee-Side Employment Attorney

"Kelly Charles-Collins has written a must-read work...it's for everyone who's ever been or will be involved in workplace investigations. This is a practical guide and valuable resource that assists the reader in resetting their thought process on investigations. This book helps in navigating the legal pitfalls internal investigations create and shows how to turn chaos into order. This is the "moment of truth" for the company to maintain and win back employee trust in the organization."

TODD YORK, GPHR, SPHR, SHRM-SCP
Sr. Global Strategic HR Advisor for Audax HR

"*Ace Your Workplace Investigations* shows you how to conduct an effective investigation, but it's much more than that. It offers great insights into creating a culture based on trust, truthfulness, and engagement so that your employees and organization can thrive. And a bonus is that author Kelly Charles-Collins' personality shines through, making the book a surprisingly fun read. I highly recommend it!"

LIBBY GILL, Executive Coach, Speaker and
Author of *The Hope-Driven Leader* and *You Unstuck*

ACE

Your
WORKPLACE
INVESTIGATIONS

*A Step-by-Step Guide for Avoiding
Friction, Covering Your Assets, and
Earning Employee Trust*

KELLY CHARLES-COLLINS, ESQ., MBA

HeartBridge Press

HeartBridge Press
PO Box 25455
Sarasota, FL 34277-2455

ISBN: 978-0-9981788-1-3

eBook ISBN: 978-0-9981788-2-0

DEDICATION

I dedicate this book to my Irie Family — husband John, son Jordan, mom Sonia, dad Teddy, sister Lisa, niece Danielle, Aunt Patsy, cousins — David, Karen, Gordon, and Dory.

You have always encouraged me to be my better self and you keep me laughing every day. I have no idea how I got so lucky to be born into this amazing village.

I am thankful every day for each one of you.

Keep loving, laughing and being Irie.

TABLE OF CONTENTS

PREFACE

Let's just tell the truth and shame the devil—employees do not trust the Human Resources (HR) Department, business owners, or management. They believe that it is useless to report anything because nothing is going to happen. "HR works for the company." Sound familiar? In some places, this might be true. But whether it is or not, it is *your*—(as owners, Human Resources personnel, managers)—responsibility to change that misconception or unfortunate reality. Conducting effective internal investigations is one way to accomplish that goal.

An "ace" is as a person who excels at an activity. I want you to be an ace at workplace investigations. Really? Yes, really. I know you would rather watch paint dry, because if you are investigating, that means there is a problem. If there is a problem, it needs to be solved. And, *you* are likely the one who must solve it. Workplace investigations are disruptive, cost time and money, and are perceived by employees, as untrustworthy. I get it. However, I guarantee if you *Ace Your Workplace Investigations*, your job will be much easier, and all these concerns will be alleviated.

In 1998, I began representing small businesses to Fortune 500 companies in employment matters, including discrimination, sexual harassment, hostile work environment, retaliation, theft, workplace violence, and you name it. I provided proactive human resources consulting and training and defended the organizations in court and

1

before administrative agencies such as the Equal Employment Opportunity Commission (EEOC).

In 2008, I began working as a Human Resources Investigator for Publix Super Markets, Inc. (Publix), a Fortune 100 company. Publix has an entire department dedicated to conducting internal investigations. I know this is not feasible for most companies, but it's not the size of the company or their budget that is important here. Rather, it's the company's focus on (1) allowing the light to shine so it can learn what is going on within the organization, (2) providing its associates the opportunity to be heard, (3) encouraging reporting, and (4) reinforcing its policies. They do this not only during an associate's employment but after. When an associate is terminated, they can appeal their termination. Those investigations are conducted with the same vigor and focus as any other investigation.

Let's revolutionize your thinking — "New HR, Who Dis?" Change your attitude about your employee complaints and workplace investigations. When your employees call you, greet them with openness and willingness. For most employees, that will be a new feeling. It will go a long way in changing their perceptions and earning their trust.

Conducting effective internal investigations is necessary for your business to continue making money. Let me repeat, conducting effective internal investigations is necessary for your business to continue making money. If you don't believe me, ask someone whose business has been affected by the #METOO and #TIMESUP movements. Disregarding problems or burying your head in the sand can be costly and detrimental and to your business, especially if you are a small business. But, it's not only the monetary costs, there are also soft costs—loss of time, goodwill, your reputation, employee mistrust, and turnover. Ask yourself, "Could my organization survive such a scandal?" If you're not sure, then this book is for you.

Your focus should not be on the process of the investigation or the time it's going to take, but rather the benefits of conducting an effective internal investigation. The years that I worked as an internal HR investigator reinforced my understanding of the importance of workplace investigations to a company's other A.C.E.— Atmosphere, Culture, and Environment.

How you handle investigations of your employees' concerns and complaints frames your employees' perceptions. Do you disregard their concerns? Do you perform a sham investigation just for the sake of saying you addressed the issue? Or do you listen to your employees' concerns, thoroughly investigate them, and take appropriate corrective action?

I'm sure you've heard the saying, "What happens in the dark, will come to the light." When you see the light, let it shine and illuminate the issues. Do not retreat into the darkness. Embrace the opportunity to find out what is going on within your business, affecting your employees' productivity, eroding employee trust, and ultimately impacting your bottom line. Stop thinking about investigations as a waste of time or a hassle — think of them as an opportunity (1) for early intervention, (2) to encourage reporting, (3) to earn employee trust, (4) to reinforce company policies, and (5) to deter the behavior.

Many people have voraciously consumed every salacious detail of the claims of sexual harassment and violence in the workplace arising out of the #METOO and #TIMESUP movements. While those details make for interesting news stories, I hope what really struck employers were the two recurring themes expressed by the women: (1) lack of reporting due to fear of retaliation and (2) the feeling that reporting would be futile. Simply put, these movements exposed a widespread mistrust of organizations, HR, owners, management, and whoever is responsible for ensuring employees feel safe in the workplace.

If you are working in fear, or running your business based on fear, how productive would you be? Ask the same question but relate it to your employees. If they are unhappy or fearful at work, they will not be productive. Who wants to produce for people or an organization they feel is not doing their best for them? Think about it — would you?

I am not saying it is all on you. HR management, at its best, is an interactive, collaborative process between management and employees driven by open communication, shared goals and mutual benefit. Employers, employees, HR personnel, and even legal counsel all have roles to play.

Employees must comply with workplace policies and timely file any complaints. Employers (owners, HR personnel, managers) must implement, communicate and consistently enforce policies, train all employees and management, ensure employees feel comfortable reporting issues, and know how to report them. And then, conduct timely, thorough and objective investigations and promptly take any necessary corrective action. Appropriately investigating all types of complaints—hostile work environment, sexual harassment or assault, discrimination, retaliation, bullying, theft, violence or other violations of organization policies, federal, state or local laws—is the organization's responsibility. Legal counsel must provide sound legal advice and work proactively with you to identify, avoid, and resolve potential issues in the workplace. This all boils down to 3 simple concepts: *Communicate, Collaborate, Cultivate.*^{SM}

* * *

An organization's Atmosphere, Culture, and Environment (A.C.E.) and its employees' perceptions of how issues and concerns are addressed, directly correlates with employee satisfaction, trust, and productivity. Remember what I said earlier: conducting effective internal investigations is essential for your business to continue making money. It is also essential for earning and maintaining employee trust.

I wrote this book for you — business owners, HR personnel, and managers — all of you who want to do the right thing. Maybe you wear all, some, or only one of those hats, or will share this information with colleagues. By reading this book and completing the exercises, you will ace the skill of conducting effective workplace investigations *and* gain the trust and respect of your employees. It's a win-win.

The facts and circumstances of each complaint and investigation you encounter will be unique and present its own set of challenges. However, your goal is to ask the right questions, uncover the relevant facts, identify areas of opportunity (e.g., lack of training), encourage reporting, intervene early, minimize legal risk to the organization, and help the organization continue making money. Accomplishing all of this, while earning employee trust by being professional, thorough, fair and consistent.

You are an integral part of your organization's team. You are a leader. Enthusiastically embrace your responsibilities. As eloquently stated by Simon Sinek[1]:

> [W]hen a leader embraces their responsibility to care for people instead of caring for numbers, then people will follow, solve problems and see to it that that leader's vision comes to life the right way, a stable way, and not the expedient way.

This is not just another CYA book that explains the steps you should take to conduct an effective workplace investigation. I believe that HR management is an interactive process. Therefore, you will not only get step-by-step directions, but we will also use a case study and exercises to demonstrate and work through the concepts.

It is generally believed that people retain more information from "what they do" as opposed to what they read, see, or hear. However, people learn in different ways. I am mostly an auditory learner, which means I learn more by listening. I am also a visual learner. Therefore, in this book, I have included a variety of methods to enhance your comprehension of the concepts being addressed.

Read this book repeatedly, until the processes become second nature. Keep it on your desk for use as a reference. Refer to it before you embark on a new investigation. Share it with others within your organization who also conduct investigations. This book is your GPS - it gives you step-by-step directions, but you still must do the work to get to your destination. By implementing the practices in this book, you will:

1. Avoid friction in your workplace
2. Cover your business' assets and
3. Earn and maintain your employees' trust.

Embrace being an "Ace."
You can do it!
Now, let's get to work.

PART I: FOUNDATION

WHY INVESTIGATE?

The price of inaction is far greater than the cost of making a mistake.

— Meister Eckhart

Have you ever told a child to do something and they asked, "Why?" I'm sure some of you are asking the same thing right now. And just like you would probably tell that child, my answer is, because I say you should. But, really, here's why. Investigations are as much a search for relevant facts as they are a mirror or magnifying glass on existing issues.

I am always a little surprised when I am asked by business owners or HR professionals if they should always do an investigation when an employee complains or they learn of an issue in the workplace, such as hostile work environment, discrimination, sexual harassment, or workplace violence. My answer is always, "YES!" If you receive a complaint from an employee or become aware of an issue, no matter how trivial it seems or how frivolous you believe it to be, you *must* investigate.

Beware of "The Trap"

Does this sound familiar? Mary-Jo – yes, Mary-Jo. That was the first name that came to mind; no idea why. But, here goes – Mary-Jo walks into your office and says:

> For the past several months, my supervisor
> has been asking me out on dates. I keep
> telling him no, but he keeps asking. Since I
> have been rejecting him, I have been given
> less desirable assignments. I also applied for
> a promotion, but he refused to interview me.
> All I want is to be left alone. I just wanted to
> tell you about it. If you could just assign me
> to another supervisor, I would be happy. I
> just want to do my work. I don't want you to
> speak to him.

Great. Happy dance — no investigation needed. Right?
Just assign Mary-Jo to another supervisor and problem
solved. WRONG! Employees may say, "I don't want you
to investigate or tell anyone about this." "I just want to
vent." "I just needed to get it off my chest." Intentionally
or unintentionally, this is a trap. *You must always
investigate.*

Why? Because as my mother used to always tell me, "It's
all fun and games until somebody loses an eye." Huh –
Kelly, what are you talking about? I mean that employees
will say that everything is fine until something negative,
such as a termination, demotion, or suspension happens, or
a friend, family member or employee gets in their ear. Then
suddenly just getting Mary-Jo a new supervisor is no longer
fine. It becomes: I told you there was a problem and you did
not investigate or do anything about it. There can be
significant consequences for failing to timely investigate a
claim or ineffectively investigating a claim.

CONSEQUENCES OF INEFFECTIVE OR UNTIMELY INVESTIGATIONS
1. Costly litigation
2. Unresolved issues
3. Loss of employee trust
4. Unavailable witnesses, lack of recollection, lost evidence

* * *

Breathe in, Breathe Out

I know, I know ... you are asking, Kelly, who has time to do that for every little complaint? You do. You must make the time. Every investigation does not have to be a full-blown, you're on the hot seat inquisition. **An investigation is a systematic or formal inquiry to discover and examine the facts to establish the truth.**[2] What a specific investigation entails and how detailed it must be will be directed by the issues raised by the complaint or other issues you become aware of.

I'm sure you've heard the sayings "happy wife, happy life" or "if momma ain't happy, nobody's happy." Same thing in the workplace. If your employees are unhappy, you and the organization will also ultimately be unhappy, which will negatively affect the organization's productivity and its bottom line. Employees can be an organization's biggest asset or their biggest liability.

"Numbers are the highest degree of knowledge. It is knowledge itself." – Plato. So, let's discuss some numbers

which are relevant to your decision about why you should investigate.

2017 EEOC CHARGE AND LITIGATION STATISTICS[3]
<ul><li>84, 254 individuals filed charges of discrimination<ul><li>This does not include charges with state or local Fair Employment Practices Agencies (FEPA)[4]</li><li>Retaliation claims were the most frequently filed, followed by race and disability</li><li>6,696 sexual harassment claims resulting in $46.3 in monetary benefits</li></ul></li><li>540,000 calls received on the EEOC toll-free number</li><li>155,000 inquiries to field offices</li><li>184 merit lawsuits filed by the EEOC<ul><li>124 individual suits</li><li>30 suits involving multiple victims or discriminatory policies</li><li>30 systemic discrimination cases</li><li>90.8% successfully resolved</li></ul></li><li>125 suits resolved</li><li>$398 million secured from private sector and state and local governments through settlements and litigation.</li></ul>

Additionally, in a 2017 study[5] on employee lawsuits conducted by Hiscox USA, a specialist insurance company:

> [a] representative study of 1,214 closed claims reported by small to medium-sized enterprises (SMEs) with fewer than 500 employees showed that 24% of employment charges resulted in **defense and settlement costs averaging** a total of **$160,000**. On average, those matters took **318 days to resolve**. (emphasis added)

Can your organization survive the $160,000.00 in defense costs and the 318 days of interruption to your business or paying out any settlements and attorneys' fees resulting from these charges?

The same study also showed that U.S. companies had a 10.5% chance of having an employment charge filed against them. That might not seem like a high likelihood, but what if your organization is one of that 10.5%?

Many of the claims filed by employees fail to make it to federal court—most settle—and of the ones that do proceed to court, only about 1% succeed.[6]

> For fiscal year 2016 (Oct. 1, 2015 through Sept. 30, 2016), employees filed 97,443 charges, and the EEOC issued 81,129 Notices to Sue (83.3%), according to records provided to *Fast Company*. For that same period, meanwhile, Lex Machina counted only 7,239 cases that went onto lawsuits—less than a tenth of the charges EEOC gave a green light to over the same time frame.

However, you should not seek comfort in this and become complacent. Whether a claim results in a lawsuit or not, the fact that a claim was filed at all, will cost you time and money.

There is no cost to an employee to file an EEOC charge. Additionally, many attorneys who represent employees in employment law matters do so on contingency. Therefore, if anything at all, an employees' out-of-pocket expenses are minimal. To the contrary, a business owner incurs attorneys' fees immediately. My experience is that attorneys who represent companies in these cases do not do so on a contingency basis. Thus, unlike employees, organizations most often immediately incur significant costs to retain competent counsel.

It is also important to understand that whether the organization wins or loses a claim filed by an employee, except in very limited circumstances, the organization cannot recoup its attorney's fees. Moreover, if the matter is settled or the organization is found liable to the employee, not only will the organization be responsible for its own attorney's fees, it will be responsible for paying the employee's attorney's fees *and* any settlement or judgment to the employee. This could range in the hundreds of thousands of dollars.

So, the next time an employee files a complaint or you become aware of an issue but do not feel like being bothered or think you don't have the time to address it, ask yourself, "Can my organization absorb this type of loss?"

* * *

BENEFITS OF INVESTIGATIONS

Trust is a fragile thing. Easy to break. Easy to lose. And one of the hardest things to ever get back.

– Unknown

Employee complaints are a cost of doing business. If you want to reduce those costs and earn and maintain employee trust, you must address employee complaints by conducting effective workplace investigations.

Workplace investigations serve several purposes: (1) to impartially address an employee's complaint or another workplace issue, (2) to determine whether any policies, rules, standards, or laws have been violated, (3) to uncover any other issues brewing in the workplace; (4) to correct inappropriate behavior, (5) to identify areas of opportunity in the business (training deficiencies, lack of awareness of policies, inconsistent application of policies), (6) to minimize legal risk to the business, and (7) to develop a plan to correct and deter the offending behavior.

There are also many benefits to conducting effective workplace investigations.

BENEFITS OF EFFECTIVE INVESTIGATIONS
1. Avoiding disruption in the workplace
2. Covering your organization's assets
3. Earning and maintaining employee trust
4. Enforcement of company policies
5. Reduction of the need for employee complaints
6. Encouragement of employees to report concerns
7. Facilitation of early intervention and early identification of opportunities

Ensuring employees feel valued, appreciated and acknowledged will reduce the need for employee complaints and create safe and inclusive workplaces, thereby minimizing legal risk to the organization and protecting the bottom line. Yes, the bottom line–at the end of it all, it is about money. But not just from the organization's perspective. When employees work they want to get paid. For them to get paid the organization needs to be profitable. The organization cannot be profitable if it is continuously paying lawyers, settlements, and judgments.

Now, don't get me wrong, I am a trial lawyer, so I will be there to help my clients pick up the pieces if a claim arises. However, I believe in a proactive approach to risk management, so I would rather be there as a trusted advisor up front, to help you keep the pieces in place.

No matter the form of the compliant–oral, written, rumor, or a discussion overheard in the hallway, *you must investigate*. You must address the issues raised. You must determine if there is any veracity to the claims. You must take any necessary, prompt, and appropriate corrective action.

It takes a lot of courage for employees to come forward and report an issue to HR. Their friends and co-workers likely already know what is happening, so they are *all* waiting to see what the organization, and particularly HR, will do. As evidenced by the #METOO movement, once one person complains, more people feel free to complain, but that also depends on how the original Complainant's situation is handled. Your job is to ensure that policies are being enforced and that your employees are working in a safe and inclusive environment.

This is your opportunity to be an ACE and dispel the myth that the HR department only cares about the organization, and not the employees.

Revolutionize your thinking. Whether you are a business owner, Human Resources professional, or member of the management team, embrace the opportunity to find out what is: going on in your business, affecting your employees' productivity, eroding employee trust, and ultimately impacting your bottom line.

* * *

THE PLAYBOOK

The best defense is a great offense.

~ Unknown

Whether your investigation will be effective is determined before you ever receive a complaint. Like a house, you must have a solid foundation. Employee handbooks are an integral part of that foundation. The handbook is a guide for your employees that sets forth their roles and responsibilities as well as the organization's expectations. It also advises employees of the organization's obligations.

For example, if an employee has a complaint, the handbook should set forth clearly who they should complain to, what the process is once the complaint is filed, generally describe how the investigation will be handled, and ensure employees that they will not be retaliated against for making a complaint. Before you read any further, ask yourself these questions:

- Does your organization have an employee handbook?

- Have your employees been provided copies of the handbook?

- Are your employees required to sign an acknowledgment of its receipt?

- Does that handbook specify what conduct is unacceptable?

- Do you have written anti-discrimination, anti-harassment and no retaliation policies?

- Are these policies posted in the workplace?

- Is your complaint process and investigation protocol in your handbook?

- Does it provide alternative avenues of reporting for employees?

- Have those policies been recently reviewed and updated?

- Has your handbook been reviewed by legal counsel?

- Have you trained your employees and management personnel about those policies?

- Have you documented that every employee and new hire received training?

- Do you have a standardized process for conducting investigations?

If your answer to any of these questions is "No," your organization's foundation is on shaky ground. An employee handbook communicates the organization's culture, mission, values, policies, procedures and expectations to employees and provides policies about boundaries for acceptable behavior. It provides information to employees on how and where to report complaints and concerns, and how those matters will be investigated.

Employee handbooks are also important tools for reinforcing an organization's commitment to complying with federal and state laws. This is particularly important in the event of an employee claim or lawsuit. If an employee files a claim for unemployment benefits, a charge of discrimination, or a lawsuit against the organization, in order to win, your attorneys must have plausible, credible defenses for the organization's actions.

Let us look at some scenarios that highlight the importance of implementing, communicating and enforcing company policies and procedures.

SCENARIO NO. 1
UNEMPLOYMENT COMPENSATION HEARING

During unemployment compensation hearings, an employer's defense is usually that the employee violated an organization policy. These are the typical questions the Unemployment Referee will ask the organization representative: (1) Do you have an employee handbook, (2) Is the policy you allege was violated in the handbook, (3) How was this policy communicated to the employee, (4) Are employees made aware of these policies in any form beyond the employee handbook, and (5) Did the employee sign a form acknowledging receipt of the employee handbook? If your answers are "yes," you are well on your way to a win. If not, get out your checkbook.

SCENARIO NO. 2
SEXUAL HARASSMENT COMPLAINT

Let's go back to Mary Jo–the same scenario where she claims she is being asked out on dates by her supervisor, given unfavorable assignments, and refused a promotion but this time Mary Jo does not complain to anyone in the organization. Mary Jo then gets terminated for poor job performance. A few weeks or months later, you receive a letter from the Equal Employment Opportunity Commission (EEOC). Mary Jo is claiming sexual harassment and

---

retaliation. WHAT??? What is Mary Jo talking about?

Here is the beginning of your organization's defense. An organization cannot correct a problem it doesn't know about. In these cases, if the organization has a written anti-harassment policy, the organization can assert the defense that it exercised reasonable care to prevent sexual harassment, and the employee unreasonably failed to take advantage of any corrective opportunities provided by the organization.

Asserting the defense is your attorney's job. Providing the offense is yours.

BE PROACTIVE

• Implement a comprehensive employee handbook that includes written anti-discrimination, anti-harassment, workplace misconduct, and anti-retaliation policies that clearly set forth:
 	
  o What conduct is prohibited
 	
  o The obligations of the organization and its supervisors to ensure a workplace free of harassment and discrimination
 	
  o The protocol and process for employees to report harassing, discriminatory, or retaliatory behavior
 	
  o The employer's procedure for investigating such claims
 	
  o Assurance that employees will not be retaliated against for filing a complaint
 	
• Publicize the policies

- Provide electronic access or printed copies of the employee handbook to all employees. Have employees sign an acknowledgement of its receipt.

- Train management and non-management employees about your organization's policies and applicable laws

- Promptly and thoroughly investigate all claims and take appropriate corrective action

- Consistently and routinely enforce policies

This is worth repeating: employers (owners, Human Resources personnel, managers) must implement, communicate, consistently enforce policies, train management and non-management employees about organization policies and applicable laws, ensure employees feel comfortable reporting issues, and know how to report these issues. Conduct timely, thorough and objective investigations. And then promptly take any necessary corrective action.

* * *

Let me digress a minute to focus a bit on the importance of training. It is wonderful to have policies in place and include them in a pretty handbook that you give to your employees during orientation. But it is not enough to just have the policies and expect that your employees will read or even understand them all. **Everyone must be trained – owners, HR personnel, managers, and non-managers.** Everyone in the company needs to know the rules and laws that govern their behavior, the organization's expectations and their roles and responsibilities.

When was the last time your employees received training on what constitutes sexual harassment, discrimination, retaliation, a hostile work environment, or violence in the workplace? If your answer is, "Never," remember this hashtag: #TIMESUP. It is imperative you begin training everyone or provide a refresher. Otherwise, your organization is in peril of becoming a news headline. This should be a no brainer. Training is a lot less expensive than litigation.

"When you know better, do better." Will training rid us of sexual harassment, discrimination, violence, or retaliation? No, but many complaints in the workplace arise from a lack of knowledge rather than a willful intent to violate a policy, rule, or law. Training your employees is a major factor in reducing those complaints and creating a safe and inclusive workplace.

Regular training of your employees is essential whether you receive complaints or not. However, if you receive a complaint, whether the claim is substantiated or not, after a thorough investigation, some level of training to reinforce organization policies should be provided to employees. Just like conducting investigations is worth the time, so is training. And they will both avoid friction, cover your assets, and earn employee trust.

* * *

ACE YOUR WORKPLACE INVESTIGATIONS:

1. Has your company employee handbook been updated within the last 6 months?

   a. If yes, calendar 6 months from today to have your handbook reviewed and/or updated by legal counsel.

   b. If no, immediately have your handbook reviewed and/or updated by legal counsel.

2. Confirm that all employees have either electronic access or a hard copy of the handbook.

3. Then verify that all current employees have signed a handbook acknowledgement and that a copy is in their personnel file. If it's not, get the employee to sign one and place it in their personnel file.

4. Have you provided anti-harassment, anti-discrimination, anti-retaliation or workplace policy violation training to your employees in the past 6 months?

5. If training has not been provided, schedule that training to be completed within the next 3 months.

* * *

NOTES

NOTES

NOTES

NOTES

PART II: PLAN

SETTING THE STAGE

*Everybody's got a different way of telling a story
— and has different stories to tell.*

–Keith Richards

We will be using the following fictitious case study to explore the many concepts involved in conducting an effective workplace investigation.

CASE STUDY
The Complainant, a non-management employee, reports to HR that she has heard from several other non-management employees (Employees X, Y, and Z) that they are being sexually harassed by the Respondent, a male Department Manager. These non-management employees told Complainant that other employees had also witnessed the incidents and Complainant said other employees have said they heard rumors about the Respondent's behavior.
Employee X claimed that the Respondent rubbed against her breasts.
Employee Y said that the Respondent grabbed her butt, sent her text messages, called her after hours and asked her personal questions that made her feel uncomfortable.
Employee Y reported the Respondent's actions to her supervisor, Manager 1. Manager 1 reported the complaint to

her direct manager, Sr. Manager 2. Manager 1 explained to Sr. Manager 2 that she believed Employee Y because the Respondent had previously done almost the same thing to her, Manager 1.

Employee Z told the Complainant that the Respondent had rubbed her shoulders and back, and she had told him to stop. He also sent her text messages, called her and asked her out for dinner and drinks.

Employees X, Y, and Z provided witness statements to Sr. Manager 2.

Prior to complaining to HR, Complainant reported these claims to her direct manager, Manager 3, who brushed off the Complainant's claims, because he did not think the Respondent had done anything inappropriate. Complainant also advised her Manager 3 that Employees X, Y, and Z did not want to be left alone to work with the Respondent, because they were in fear of what he would do to them.

After the Complainant reported these claims to Manager 3, she began experiencing negative treatment from the Respondent: He began speaking badly about her to vendors, customers, and other employees. He made comments about her age and her family and claimed her job performance was poor. He also told other employees he wanted to fire the Complainant.

Is your head spinning — trying to keep track of who, what, where, and when? Get used to it. That is generally how this happens. Complaints are rarely as straightforward as he said, she said. There are sometimes several versions, many moving parts and witnesses, different locations and dates, and a variety of types of physical evidence. Even investigations that begin simply, may evolve into a hornet's nest.

To conduct an effective investigation, you must be able to keep all this straight. Be able to identify all the issues involved as well as develop a plan for conducting a thorough and fair investigation. Have no fear, we will help you with this in the following pages of this book.

* * *

PLANNING THE INVESTIGATION

"If you fail to plan, you are planning to fail."
                                    –Benjamin Franklin

Assuming your employee handbook has been drafted, it's been reviewed by counsel and communicated to your employees, let's jump right into how to plan an investigation.

To effectively investigate you must have a plan. Develop a standardized investigation process, i.e., the plan you will always follow when investigating.

A standardized plan has several benefits. First, it will save time, be less disruptive to the organization and make investigations more effective. If there is a process, particularly an automated one, you will not be recreating the wheel for every investigation. Second, in the event of litigation, a standardized process will more easily withstand scrutiny by the court and an employee's attorney. Third, a standardized plan will ensure consistency — no matter who is conducting the investigation, it should be done the same way.

A note of caution — there is no "standard" timeframe for conducting an investigation. The length of an investigation is dictated by the circumstances — the issues raised; necessity for pre-investigation actions; the number, location, and availability of witnesses; and involvement of outside parties, such as attorneys, third-party consultants, board of directors, etc.

NECESSARY FACTORS IN DEVELOPING STANDARDIZED PROCESS
• Complaint intake
• Identification and assessment of issues
• Pre-investigation actions
• Selection of the right investigator
• Conducting interviews
o Identification of necessary witnesses
o Order of witness interviews
o Handling requests for representation and/or ability to record the interview
o Gathering documents or other physical evidence
o Gag orders or confidentiality policy
• Evaluating evidence
• Drafting the final report
• Communication of findings
• Taking necessary corrective action
• Retaining and Disposing Evidence

* * *

ACE YOUR WORKPLACE INVESTIGATIONS:

1. Where do you look to determine what issues are being raised by the Complainant?
2. Is your investigation process standardized? If not, what processes do you need to put in place to make it standardized?
3. Determine if your state has its own employment discrimination law. If so, what are the protected categories?
4. Does the county/city where your organization is located have employment discrimination laws? If so, what are the protected categories? City and county ordinances can be found at https://library.municode.com.

* * *

NOTES

NOTES

NOTES

NOTES

PART III – PREPARE

ANALYZING THE COMPLAINT

The goal is to turn data into information, and information into insight.

–Carly Fiorina

Has as an employee, like the Complainant, filed an oral or written complaint with a supervisor or your Human Resources department? Was a complaint called into a hotline or submitted online? Did you receive a charge of discrimination, demand letter or a lawsuit? What's next? Getting familiar with each part of a standardized plan, using our sample case study as an example. Let's get started.

Document the Complaint

Take very detailed notes and ask clarifying questions. You want to ensure that you have as much information from the Complainant as you can gather before beginning your investigation. Either you or the Complainant can document the complaint, in writing, on a standard form or other type of document. See Illustration No. 1 for Sample Employee Complaint Intake Form.

Illustration No. 1

SAMPLE EMPLOYEE COMPLAINT INTAKE FORM

Date: _____

Complainant Name & Title:

_____

Respondent Name & Title:

_____

Name of person taking complaint:

_____

Date of incident(s): _____

Location of incident(s):

_____

Description of incident(s):

_____

_____

_____

Names and contact information of witnesses:

_____

_____

Have you reported this incident(s) to anyone: ____ Yes ____No

If yes, provide name and title of person reported to and date:

_____

Page 1 of 2

SAMPLE EMPLOYEE COMPLAINT INTAKE FORM (con't)

Identify any physical evidence you believe supports your claim and the location of any such evidence:

_____

_____

_____

Resolution Requested:

_____

_____

_____

Additional Comments:

_____

_____

_____

_____

I acknowledge that I have read this document and understand my obligation to provide information as needed and to cooperate fully and completely with any investigation of this complaint. Should it become necessary, I authorize the company to disclose my identity and/or details of this complaint.

Your signature: _____ Date: _____

Your email address:_____

Your phone number: _____

Intake Representative name and title: _____

Representative signature: _____ Date: _____

Page 2 of 2

If you are completing the intake form, take very precise and detailed notes. If the Complainant completes the intake form or other document, make sure to read it, ensure that everything is legible and if not, make it legible before the Complainant leaves. Additionally, clarify information in the complaint. Often, employees will refer to employees only by their first names, or use pronouns as he, she, them. You will need to gather more specific information before beginning your investigation. Using our case study on pages 32-33, here are examples of clarifications you should request:

1. Complete names and positions of Employees X, Y, and Z.
2. Names of any other witnesses who overheard rumors about the Respondent.
3. Specific dates incidents allegedly occurred.
4. Current location of the written statements.
5. Dates that Complainant and Employee X, Y, and Z's complained to management.
6. Responses by management to the complaints.
7. Ask the Complainant what their expectations are and how they would like to see the matter resolved.

Identify and Assess the Issues Raised by the Complaint

The scope of the investigation will be determined by the issues raised in the complaint and the company policies, rules, or laws that may have been violated. Issues are your GPS. Identifying the issues(s) will determine the scope and nature of the investigation. Unless you know what you are looking for, you have no idea where to look. You need to know what additional information you will need to substantiate or negate the claims.

There are many federal and state law claims that could arise from misconduct of managers, non-managers, customers and vendors. While state law claims differ from state to state, here is a sample and brief explanation of the more common types of claims you will encounter.

FEDERAL LAWS
Age Discrimination in Employment Act (ADEA) – discriminating against employees over the age of 40
American with Disabilities Act (ADA) – discriminating against and/or failing to accommodate a person with a qualified disability
Equal Pay Act (EPA) – paying one gender less than another gender for the same work
Fair Labor Standards Act (FLSA) – failure to pay employees minimum wage or overtime, misclassification of employees, child labor violations
Family and Medical Leave Act (FMLA) – failing to provide leave and/or retaliating against an employee for requesting or taking leave for their or a covered family member's serious health condition
Occupational Safety & Health Administration Law (OSHA) – workplace safety claims
Pregnancy Discrimination Act (PDA) – discriminating and/or retaliating against or failing to accommodate a pregnant employee
Title VII of the Civil Rights Act of 1964 (Title VII) – harassing, discriminating and/or retaliating against an employee based on certain protected categories

STATE LAW CLAIMS

Assault – a verbal or non-physical threat of violence

Battery – unlawful or unwanted touching

Negligent Hiring – hiring an employee whose previous history of inappropriate behavior would have easily been discovered had the employer exercised due diligence

Negligent Retention – continuing to employ an employee after you learn of or have reason to know the employee has engaged in inappropriate behavior

Negligent Supervision – failing to properly supervise an employee you know or have reason to know has engaged in inappropriate behavior

If you have identified that a specific company policy may have been violated, what conduct has the organization historically considered was a violation of that policy? If you believe that a federal or state law may have been violated, do you know what is needed to properly evaluate the claim? If not, you should seek legal counsel.

Pre-Investigation Actions

Depending on the type of issue(s) raised by the complaint, some pre-investigation actions may need to be taken. For example, if the claim is one of sexual harassment or violence, consider whether you need to separate the Complainant from the Respondent in the workplace. There are several ways this can be accomplished:

- Transfer or reassign the parties

- Change schedules

- If the Respondent is the Complainant's manager, assign the Complainant to a new manager or

- Place the Respondent or Complainant on leave, paid or unpaid, during the investigation.

Removing either party from the workplace should be a final resort and only done if there is no other alternative. Placing either party on leave will have some administrative implications for the organization. Also, be mindful that transferring the Complainant or placing him/her on leave involuntarily may raise other issues, such as retaliation. Thus, to minimize the risk of exposure down the road, employers should seek legal advice prior to taking any of these pre-investigation actions.

A little heads up, at the end of your investigation, you must complete a final report of your findings. If you want a sneak peak of what that entails, see Illustration No. 3 – Sample Investigation Report on pages 126-128.

Before we move forward, let's recap. You have met with the Complainant, documented the complaint, clarified the information in the complaint, identified any potential violations of company policy, federal or state law, and taken any pre-investigation actions. You are now ready to select your investigator.

* * *

ACE YOUR WORKPLACE INVESTIGATIONS:

1. You receive the complaint in our case study on pages 32-33, what are the first two things you need to do?

   a. What additional information do you need from the Complainant before you start your investigation?

   b. What, if any, pre-investigation actions should you take?

2. Using your employee handbook and our case study on pages 32-33, identify any workplace policies that may have been violated.

3. Identify any federal or state laws that may have been violated in our case study.

* * *

NOTES

NOTES

NOTES

NOTES

SELECTING THE INVESTIGATOR

I have no special talents. I am only passionately curious.

—Albert Einstein

Selecting the right, impartial investigator is vital to your employees' perception of the integrity of the investigation process and your organization. I'm sure you have heard employees say things like, "Nothing is going to happen, HR staff only care about protecting the organization." The unfortunate truth is that there is a perception amongst many employees that Human Resources staff and managers are biased in favor of the organization. It is your job to overcome that perception. Selecting the right, impartial investigator is one of the ways you can dispel this myth.

Some people believe the way to eliminate this bias is to always hire an outside investigator, such as outside counsel. However, simply bringing in an outside investigator is not the magic pill. Organizations must work to build a culture of trust among their employees, way before the need for an investigation. If that is the culture that is cultivated, employees will have faith that the investigation, no matter who does it, will be done with professionalism and integrity.

Third-Party Investigators

Keep in mind that there may be situations where the right investigator will be an outside consultant or an attorney. For example, if the complaint involves the owner, a C-Suite executive (e.g., president, vice-president, chief financial officer, chief executive officer), or a board member, you should seriously consider using an attorney or outside counsel. Conducting an unbiased investigation of such high-level personnel can be difficult. If you are ever uncertain about your own ability or that of anyone else in the organization to conduct an unbiased investigation, you should consult with legal counsel. It's better to be safe than sorry.

Additionally, if you do decide to have a third-party conduct an investigation, you should be aware of the requirements of the Fair and Accurate Credit Transactions Act of 2003 (FACTA). You can retain a third-party to conduct workplace investigations without first notifying the target of the investigation or obtaining their consent.

Time may also be a consideration. If your organization cannot timely investigate a claim, you should highly consider outsourcing the investigation. Delaying an investigation is unacceptable and can be costly if the claim proceeds to litigation.

If you decide to use a third-party investigator or an attorney, here are some things to be aware of:

1. Participate in selecting who the investigator is. You know your employees and workplace better than anyone. You will have a better sense of the personality that would mesh with your workforce.

2. While your attorney's notes and work product, such as reports, are likely privileged, your attorney will

likely be a witness in any litigation proceeding and may be barred from representing the organization at trial.

3. Any outside consultant is an agent of the organization and therefore must conduct the investigation in accordance with the organization's policies and guidelines. The same considerations and safeguards that I have explained above should be employed by the organization during an in-house investigation and should be insisted upon if you decide to use an outside consultant or an attorney.

4. Make sure employees clearly understand that the attorney or investigator represents the organization, not the Complainant or the Respondent.

5. Using an attorney or a third-party investigator can be costly but depending on the circumstances may be money very well spent.

In-House Investigations

For purposes of this book, let's assume you are going to conduct the investigation in-house. To the extent you can, designate a specific department, such as HR, to conduct all investigations. If you do not have an HR department, try using the highest-ranking management member. If you feel uncomfortable selecting that person, you should seek legal counsel. I would not recommend the owner of the organization conduct the investigation for several reasons — it may be difficult for the owner to remain unbiased, this exposes the owner to extensive questioning about not only the complaint but the business during litigation, and the owner needs to run the business and continue making money.

Determine whether the investigator should be a male or female. If a female employee is complaining of sexual harassment by a male employee, it is probably better to have a female investigator. If a male employee is being Respondent of physical violence, it may be better to have a male investigator. Obviously, these are generalities. Evaluate each situation to determine what would make the employee more comfortable or create a safe environment for conducting interviews.

Should the investigator always be the same person or the person who holds a specific position (e.g. HR Manager)? Do you need an investigator who has specific expertise, e.g. computer forensics or workplace violence? And this should go without saying, but I will say it anyway, you know I need to state the obvious — the Respondent should not have any direct or indirect control over the investigation or the investigator. To Moreover, to the extent possible, investigators should also refrain from communicating outside the process with anyone who is or may be directly involved in the matters being investigate, or with anyone who is or may be interviewed.

You need an investigator who is available, thorough, trained (by someone like me, another attorney, or a trained professional), impartial, discrete and yes, "nosy." How do you determine whether someone has these qualities? Observation of how they handle their day-to-day responsibilities and how they interact with colleagues and employees. Or you may want to have one or more your employees trained to conduct workplace investigations.

When asked how I know what questions to ask, I say one must be inquisitive, curious, and "nosy." The right investigator will want to know what happened next and the who, when, what, and why of every complaint. You must get ALL the relevant information. The investigator cannot be afraid to ask probing questions, be afraid to address sensitive or explicit topics, or be afraid of confrontation. In some situations, if you are the investigator, you may hear some things that will make you blush.

Practice your poker face. Learn not to react. Maintain your composure. Do not jump to conclusions or be judgmental. Just as you are observing theirs, the witness is observing your body language, which I discuss later. Your body language, tone, and attitude could play a role in the perception of whether you are biased. If you react negatively or aggressively, they may shut down. If they perceive that you think they are being evasive or untruthful, they may get defensive. Remember, your job is to gather as much relevant information as possible. So, you want the Complainant, Respondent, and witnesses to feel comfortable telling you everything they know.

FACTORS FOR SELECTING AN IMPARTIAL INVESTIGATOR

- Knowledgeable about organization policies and employment law issues.

- Impartial, well-respected, and credible.

- Able to communicate with employees at all levels of the organization.

- Trustworthy and able to keep information confidential.

- Well-organized and able to follow the standardized plan.

- Able to objectively gather and consider the relevant facts.

- Well-trained in interviewing skills and evaluating credibility.

- Not afraid to ask tough questions and challenge witnesses' accounts of events.

- An active listener who can react in real-time to information being provided and follow-up.

* * *

ACE YOUR WORKPLACE INVESTIGATIONS:

1. Does your organization have a specific department that conducts all investigations?

2. Prior to reading this chapter of the book, how has your organization selected the person who investigated employee claims?

3. Who in your organization would you consider having the attributes of a good investigator?

4. Has the person(s) received training on how to conduct effective workplace investigations?

5. Do you have outside employment counsel you can consult about sensitive investigations or investigations you are uncertain about?

6. Using our case study on pages 32-33:

a. What factors would you consider important for the person selected to investigate the Complainant's claims?

b. Do you have any concerns about who should/could investigate these claims?

c. Should this investigation be handled in-house or by outside counsel or a consultant? Why or Why not?

* * *

NOTES

NOTES

NOTES

NOTES

NOTES

Determining the Lineup

Who's on first?

−Abbott & Costello

Now that the investigator has been selected, it is time to determine the witness lineup. As you see from our case study, the investigator may be required to interview quite a few witnesses and because of the many claims, the order of the interviews might be strategically important. Let's discuss how to handle these issues.

Who Are the Necessary Witnesses

Before interviews are conducted, it must first be determined who to interview. Begin with reviewing the complaint. Were any witnesses named in the complaint? Were any potential witnesses referred to? Based on the allegations, are there any other witnesses that could have relevant information, e.g. other employees working in the same department or for the Respondent?

Regardless of what is in the complaint, the following people should be interviewed in every investigation:

- Complainant
- Respondent
- Supervisors
- Witnesses identified by other witnesses or in relevant documents
- People who the Complainant or Respondent have asked you to interview

- Third parties who could reasonably be expected to have relevant information

This last category may seem a little vague. Who potentially falls into this category? Let me explain by way of example. Imagine that your organization's hours are 9am – 5pm. However, you have some employees that work after hours, finishing a project, or like me just prefer to come in later and work later. That employee files a complaint that they are being harassed by their supervisor.

During your interview, you learn that this alleged harassment occurs not only during regular business hours, but also after hours, when other employees have already gone home. At first blush, you may think that regarding those "after hours" allegations, you have a he said/she said situation. That may or may not be true. Does your organization have an after-hours cleaning crew? Is there security in the building? Are any maintenance people around after-hours? Those individuals are the types of "third parties" who could reasonably be expected to have relevant information. You never know what they may have heard or seen as they go about their work.

Think broadly about who a potential witness may be. Then narrow your focus by considering the circumstances and their opportunity to have heard or witnessed anything that would be relevant to the issues you are investigating. Interview all those people and because they are likely not under your control, try to secure a written statement and all relevant contact information.

Who Do You Interview First, Next ...

The investigation will have been preceded by a complaint or some other issue. The Complainant should be your first witness. But who do you interview next? Your instinct may be to immediately interview the Respondent. However, doing so may not be the most strategic move based on the circumstances. If based on the allegations, you have any concerns that the Respondent may not be forthcoming unless confronted with facts, you may want to first get corroborating information from other potential witnesses. Likewise, if you have questions about the Complainant's complaint, speaking with others who would have the ability to corroborate or negate the claim may assist your evaluation and guide your interview of the Respondent.

This is really a strategic decision – like playing a game of chess. But do not despair. If you are not sure what order to interview witnesses, just ensure that you interview all potential witnesses so that you are able to make a well-reasoned decision. And remember, you may have to interview witnesses more than once.

***

ACE YOUR WORKPLACE INVESTIGATIONS

1. Using our case study example on pages 32-33:

    a.   Identify the Complainant.

    b.   Identify any other potential Complainants.

    c.   Identify the Respondent.

    d.   Identify any supervisors.

    e.   Identify any potential third-party witnesses.

2. List the order in which you would interview these witnesses.

* * *

NOTES

NOTES

NOTES

NOTES

Preparing for Witness Interviews

Proper planning and preparation prevents poor performance.

–Stephen Keague

There are several types of interview techniques and strategies, most of which originated in the context of criminal investigations and are based on interrogating witnesses. *Your job is to interview, <u>not</u> interrogate.* What's the difference? Interviews are non-accusatory, and their purpose is to gather relevant information. Interrogations are accusatory and involve active persuasion to seek the truth. Your job in conducting workplace investigations is to interview witnesses to gather the relevant facts to allow you to make a sound decision about whether it is more likely than not that the conduct complained of occurred. Do not prejudge. Go where the relevant facts lead you.

Prepare

Review all information in your possession prior to your first interview. As we discussed earlier, make sure you understand what is necessary to establish that any organization policy, federal or state law that is claimed to have been violated, or may be violated based on the issues raised by the complaint. If you unsure, seek legal advice.

This will guide the questions you ask the witnesses. Writing out questions in advance is not required. However, doing so will help keep you on track, ensure that you cover everything you intended to cover, and will help with comparing and contrasting answers received from the witnesses.

You must be the most knowledgeable person in the room, or at the very least know enough to allow you to portray that you are. The more you know, the better able you are to build a rapport and probe inconsistencies.

Location of Interviews

To the extent possible, interviews should be conducted in-person, in a closed office environment where employees feel comfortable speaking without fear of being seen or heard by others. There should be no obstacles to the employee being able to voluntarily leave the room at any time. Employees should be seated closest to the door.

If a witness is a former employee or is not available in-person, it is appropriate to conduct the interview by phone or video-conference (e.g., Skype or Zoom). Video-conferencing is preferable so that you can observe the witness.

Handling Employee Requests for Representation

Employees may ask to have a representative or witness present for the interview. Generally, because you are not required to allow such representation, best practice is to deny the request. However, if your workforce is unionized, the collective bargaining agreement may require the presence of a representative, such as a union steward.

Also, depending on the circumstances of the case, the investigator may want to have a witness present during interviews. If the witness is a female and the investigator is a male, best practice would be to have another female present as a witness to the interview. The witness could take notes during the interview or simply be present as an eye-witness to the interview.

Handling Employee Requests to Electronically Record the Interview

Employees may ask if they can electronically record the interview. Recording of telephone calls or in-person conversations (including recording video that captures sound) may be limited by federal and state wiretapping laws.[7] The most important issue is whether you need consent from one or all parties before recording it. Federal law and some states allow recording in one party consents; other states require all parties to consent. This could present an issue if the parties are in different states.

In states where "one-party consent" is allowed, that means if an employee is a witness to a conversation, they can record it. If the employee is not a party to the conversation, in a "one-party consent" state, they can record the conversation or phone call if one source consents and has full knowledge that the communication will be recorded.

Several states have "two-party consent" laws — California, Connecticut, Delaware, Florida, Illinois, Maryland, Massachusetts, Michigan, Montana, Nevada, New Hampshire, Oregon, Pennsylvania, Vermont, and Washington. "Two-party consent" means that consent must be obtained from every party (if more than two involved) to the phone call or conversation. In some states, it may be sufficient, even without verbal consent, if all parties have knowledge of the recording and proceed with the conversation.

Whether you are in a one-party or two-party state, you can refuse to be recorded. Thus, general practice is to deny any request to electronically record interviews. You should also not electronically record the interviews.

With the technology on smartphones, employees may try to circumvent your denial. Therefore, you may want to request that an employee not bring their phone into the interview. It's worth noting that if they do record without your consent, federal and state laws make disclosure of such contents illegal. To avoid any confusion, I would recommend having a written policy prohibiting any such recordings in the workplace. Below is some sample policy language:

> Due to the potential for issues such as invasion of privacy, sexual harassment and loss of productivity, as well as inappropriate disclosure of confidential information, no employee may use a camera phone function on any phone on company property or while performing work for the Company.

> The use of tape recorders, dictaphones or other types of voice recording devices anywhere on Company property, including to record conversations or activities of other employees or management, or while performing work for the Company, is also strictly prohibited, unless the device was provided to you by the Company and is used solely for legitimate business purposes.

Something else to consider, if you have a unionized workforce, look to the collective bargaining agreement to determine if there are any rules regarding electronic recording of interviews.

Confidentiality and Gag Orders

Inevitably, the Complainant, the Respondent or a witness will ask you if the investigation will be confidential. If Complainant's believe that their claims will become widely known, they may be more reluctant to come forward. Likewise, witnesses may be reluctant to cooperate for fear of retaliation. Organizations would prefer to keep these matters confidential to protect the integrity of the investigation. If employees can freely discuss what they have heard or been told during the investigation, this may increase the chances of fabrication or false corroboration. Thus, for years, requiring confidentiality and imposing gag orders was commonplace during investigations.

However, employers can no longer issue these blanket edicts. Why? Because, the National Labor Relations Board (NLRB) and the EEOC believe such blanket edicts violate employees' rights.

In the case of Banner Health Systems,[8] — an unfair labor practices case — a document relating to a requirement of confidentiality were obtained by the NLRB from Banner Health. Specifically, there was a confidentiality agreement that Banner Health required all new hires to sign. The confidentiality agreement directed Banner Health workers to not discuss their co-workers, "private employee information (such as salaries, disciplinary action, etc.)" unless the information was "shared by the employee." The agreement further stated that "[k]eeping this kind of information private and confidential is so important that if I fail to do so, I understand that I could be subject to corrective action, including termination and possibly legal action."

The NLRB found the agreement to be overbroad and impermissibly violated Banners' employees' Section 7 and 8 rights by barring them from sharing information about salaries and employee discipline.

> Section 7 of the National Labor Relations Act (the Act) guarantees employees "the right to self-organization, to form, join, or assist labor organizations, to bargain collectively through representatives of their own choosing, and to engage in other concerted activities for the purpose of collective bargaining or other mutual aid or protection," as well as the right "to refrain from any or all such activities." Section 8(a)(1) of the Act makes it an unfair labor practice for an employer "to interfere with, restrain, or coerce employees in the exercise of the rights guaranteed in Section 7" of the Act.[9]

The Board also determined that Banner unlawfully maintained a categorical policy of asking employees not to discuss certain kinds of human resources investigations. It is important to understand that Section 7 rights apply to union and non-unionized settings.

So, what can you do if you want to keep an investigation confidential? If you determine that you want employees to keep an investigation confidential, you must be able to demonstrate why that specific investigation needs to be confidential. In other words, you must be able to articulate that there is a "legitimate and substantial business justification, such as:

- For the protection of a witness for whom disclosure may endanger them.

- Evidence is in danger of being destroyed.

- Testimony is at risk of being fabricated.

- Danger of witness being coerced.

- There is a need to prevent a cover-up.

- Any other comparably serious threat exists to the integrity of an employer investigation that would be sufficient to justify a confidentiality requirement.

These cannot be generalized statements. You must be able to demonstrate objectively reasonable grounds for your determination that confidentiality is necessary.

It's worth noting that there has been discussion that this decision may be overturned. However, as of the publishing of this book, that has not happened. Thus, organizations must be careful when conducting investigations.

And what exactly is the EEOC's issue? Good question. While the NLRB is concerned with protecting an employee's statutory rights to discuss the terms and conditions of their employment, the EEOC is focused on the employer's conduct in handling the investigation itself, not the Complainant or witnesses. Remember, EEOC guidance is not the law. However, as the agency responsible for enforcing employment laws such as Title VII and the ADA, organizations must be aware of the EEOC's positions and conform their behavior where feasible and in accordance with established law.

The EEOC's *"Enforcement Guidance on Vicarious Employer Liability for Unlawful Harassment by Supervisors"*[10] provides that:

An employer should make clear to employees that it will protect the confidentiality of harassment allegations to the extent possible. An employer cannot guarantee complete confidentiality, since it cannot conduct an effective investigation without revealing certain information to the alleged harasser and potential witnesses. However, information about the allegation of harassment should be shared only with those who need to know about it. Records relating to harassment complaints should be kept confidential on the same basis.

While there may be good reasons for wanting to keep claims involving, for example, sexual harassment or assault, confidential, an individualized determination must be made. The investigator should document the specific facts and circumstances that lead to the conclusion that confidentiality is needed to protect the integrity of the investigation.

Confused? Let me break it down for you:

BOTTOM LINE: CONFIDENTIALITY
<ul><li>Do not guarantee confidentiality.</li><li>Blanket policies mandating confidentiality can be problematic.</li><li>When developing your investigation strategy, if you determine confidentiality is required, set forth in writing the specific factors (e.g., witness safety or likelihood of destruction of evidence) justifying the legitimate business justification for confidentiality.</li></ul>

Maintain this document in the investigation file.

- If a gag order is necessary, narrowly tailor it to achieve the legitimate business justification. Additionally, limit the timeframe to the pendency of the investigation.

- If you cannot justify a gag order, take reasonably necessary precautions to ensure the integrity of the investigation. For example, share only necessary information during witness interviews, limit disclosure of information to people on a need-to-know basis, or conduct interviews as close to each other as possible to reduce the opportunity for witnesses to fabricate and/or share information.

- Continue to assure complainants that their complaints will be taken seriously, that the organization will conduct a thorough and prompt investigation, and that to the extent possible, the complaint will be kept confidential.

* * *

ACE YOUR WORKPLACE INVESTIGATIONS

1. Using our case study as an example, if you received a similar complaint, where in your organization would you conduct witness interviews?

2. Does your organization have the capacity to do video conferences if necessary?

3. One of the witnesses in our case study asks permission to have a representative present during

the interview and you have decided to deny her request. Write out how you will explain your decision.

4. Employee X, in our case study, asks permission to record her interview and you have decided to deny her request. Write out how you will explain your decision to employee X.

5. Using our case study, assume that you have decided this investigation needs to be confidential. List 3 specific factors that you would use to support your decision.

* * *

NOTES

NOTES

NOTES

NOTES

PART IV: EXECUTE

Conducting
the Interviews

Ask the right questions ... uncover the facts.
–Kelly Charles-Collins

Remember, this is an interview, not an interrogation. Interview suggests a dialogue where information is provided voluntarily. Whereas an interrogation suggests a one-sided examination or grilling, where information is provided due to possible coercion.

Interview Technique

Based on this distinction, the interview technique that best lends itself to workplace investigations is the PEACE[11] model.

PEACE INTERVIEW MODEL
Preparation and planning – prepare and plan for the interview **E**ngage and explain – build rapport with the witness **A**ccount – obtain the witnesses' description of events **C**losure – summarize information and provide the witness opportunity to clarify, correct or add information **E**valuate – analyze the information gathered in context of the complaint/issues raised

The PEACE model was developed in Britain and was the result of a collaboration between police officers, lawyers and psychologists. The end goal of the PEACE model is to gather relevant information.

Interviews Can Make or Break an Investigation or Case

Interviews take planning. Interviewing witnesses may seem like an easy task, but I assure you it is not. Remember, we defined "investigate" as a systematic or formal inquiry to discover and examine the facts to establish the truth. Effective interviews involve asking the right questions, actively listening to the responses, and following up in real-time on information being provided. It also involves taking detailed, accurate notes. If you are uncomfortable simultaneously asking questions, actively listening, following up and documenting what you are being told, you should have another supervisor, manager, or HR staff person present to take notes.

Do not interview witnesses in groups. You want to elicit each witnesses' own independent recollection of the events. Try to interview witnesses close in time to each other, preferably on the same day. This will reduce the opportunity for collaboration or fabrication. Allow witnesses to take breaks or leave if requested.

Engage in active listening. Active listening is a communication technique that requires that the listener fully concentrate, understand, respond and then remember what is being said. This includes observing the witnesses' behavior and body language. When used properly, active listening results in people opening up, it avoids misunderstandings, resolves conflicts, and builds trust.

You should also listen for what is not being said. Listen for why things are being said. Is there any potential bias? Is the witness alerting you to other issues? Follow up on general statements that may just be thrown out nonchalantly. For example, statements such as:

- That's just how they are or how it is

- That's nothing new

- Everybody knows that

- They are like that with everybody

- I thought HR, or the organization already knew that

These types of statements should alert you that there may be other issues brewing or that the issues being complained of have been ongoing.

Your goal is to gather as much relevant information as possible. You will be surprised how much information you get if you just let people speak. I like to ask witnesses to "Tell me what happened" and just let them go. I don't interrupt. I let them go if they continue to speak. While they are speaking, I actively listen to every word and take mental and written notes of areas to follow-up on. When they are finished, I may pause for a couple of seconds to see if they say anything else. Then, I go back through their story piece by piece, clarifying, questioning, and following-up to ensure I have a complete understanding.

Observe Everything

To effectively read body language, you need to have a baseline of the witnesses' body language. You can establish this baseline by observing the witness as you ask the preliminary questions discussed below. You can then assess any change in body language as the interview proceeds.

Notice what is and is not being said; how is it being said; watch the witnesses' body language. Use these observations to your advantage when you are interviewing the witness. There are some general characteristics we associate with certain types of body language. However, be careful that you are not misinterpreting someone's body language that is the result of their cultural background.

INTERPRETING BODY LANGUAGE
Engaged/Open
• Leaning forward
• Head tilted to one side
• Open arms
• Maintaining eye contact
• Smiling
Nervous/Shy
• Sweating
• Biting nails
• Fidgeting
• Excessive hand movements
• Lack of eye contact
Evasive/Untruthful
• Looking down or looking around
• Hand covering mouth
• Touching ear, face, nose
• Speaking quickly (if not the person's normal speaking pattern)

Silence is golden. If you feel that someone is being evasive, not telling you everything you know they know, or is being untruthful, be silent. Some people hate silence; it scares them. If your witness is one of these types, have no fear, they will fill the air. You will be surprised at the type of information they will cough up just from a few seconds of silence. However, do not unnecessarily sit in silence or sit silently for an unreasonable amount of time. Use your silence strategically.

Ask Open-Ended Questions

Your goal is to gather information. An open-ended question is one that calls for a narrative response. Closed-ended or leading questions result in a "yes" or "no" response. Since your job is to gather information, you can see why leading questions would be counterproductive to your goal. You would be telling the story, rather than the witnesses. If you find yourself speaking more than the witness, you are likely asking closed-ended or leading questions. You should be listening more than speaking. Keep asking questions until you feel you have all the information you need from the witness. You can start with a broad question and keep narrowing down until there's nothing "next."

Asking the following preliminary questions will help to relax the employee and establish a baseline for you to observe their behavior (e.g. eye contact, tone of voice, speech pattern, body movements) when they are being truthful and/or cooperative:

1. What is your position?
2. How long have you held that position?
3. Who is your supervisor or manager?

4. Have you held any other positions?

5. How long have you worked for the organization?

The following are some open-ended questions you can use whether you are interviewing the Complainant, the Respondent or a fact witness:

1. What happened?

2. What happened next?

3. Why did they do that?

4. Explain to me how the incident happened?

5. Describe in detail each act that you believe the Respondent committed that you believe to be inappropriate.

6. When you reported the incident to your supervisor, what was the response?

7. How would you like this situation resolved?

8. Who witnessed these incidents?

9. When did the incident(s) occur?

10. What type of documentation do you have to support your claim(s)?

11. Asking the right questions not only uncovers the relevant facts but can elicit essential information about the claims and corroborate or negate the claims raised. To the contrary, asking the wrong questions or poorly asking questions could lead to gathering incorrect or incomplete facts. A poorly performed investigation could result in significant damage to the organization if this matter proceeds to litigation.

Initial Interview of The Complainant

SAMPLE QUESTIONS FOR THE COMPLAINANT
1. Describe what happened.
2. Was physical contact involved? Describe it and/or demonstrate it.
3. How often has this happened?
4. Where did this happen?
5. When did this happen?
6. How long did this behavior continue?
7. Has the behavior stopped? When?
8. How did you respond to these actions?
9. Explain how the Respondent reacted to your response.
10. Were there any witnesses? What are their names and what did that person(s) witness?
11. Have you reported this to anyone in management? To whom and when? How did they respond?
12. Did you report this to anyone else? To whom and when? How did they respond?
13. Do you have any physical evidence to support your claims? What do you have?
14. Do you know why this occurred?

Interviewing Fact Witnesses

When interviewing fact witnesses, other than the Complainant, you want to gain their trust; make them feel comfortable. Ask them some general questions first, such as their job title, job duties–get them talking. Remember, this is not an interrogation. They are not the subject of the complaint. You want to encourage them to be open and honest. Begin the interview by explaining to the witness, generally, the reason for the investigation (including then names of the Complainant and the Respondent), their role as a witness, how the information will be used, any degree of confidentiality that is required, and an assurance they will not be retaliated against. Here's a sample opening statement:

> I am investigating some claims of inappropriate behavior in the workplace and I want to ask you and other employees about what you might know. To ensure we do a thorough investigation, it is essential that you are honest and that you answer my questions completely and not withhold any information. You will not be retaliated against for participating in this investigation. If at any time you are not sure what is being asked, please let me know. Do you have any questions before we begin? Will you agree to tell the truth and provide complete answers to my questions?

If you have determined that the investigation must be confidential, you should advise the witness that your discussions with them must be kept confidential and failure to do so could jeopardize the investigation. You may also tell them that they could be subject to disciplinary action for failure to follow your instructions regarding confidentiality.

* * *

The best witness is an eyewitness. However, be mindful of any relationships between the witness and the Respondent to assess any potential bias or hidden agendas.

SAMPLE QUESTIONS FOR FACT WITNESSES

1. Are you aware of any inappropriate behavior in the workplace? If yes, please explain. If they answer no, ask a more specific question – Are you aware of any inappropriate behavior between the Complainant and the Respondent? You may then need to get even more specific and provide details of the claims made.

2. Describe the behavior.

3. When and where did it occur?

4. Who was involved?

5. What did each person say or do?

6. Were there any other witnesses? Who?

7. How do you know about this behavior?

8. Did you report this behavior to anyone in management? To whom and when?

9. What was that person's response to your report?

10. What was your response to the Respondent's behavior?

11. Do you have any documents (e.g., photos, videos, text messages, Facebook posts) regarding these allegations?

12. What conversations did you have with Complainant or Respondent about these allegations? When did this occur? What did they say and/or do in response?

Witnesses may shed light on the issues raised by the Complainant or other issues that are occurring in the workplace. Do not dismiss those new claims because they are unrelated to the Complainant's original claim. You may need to begin a separate investigation—because remember, you must investigate everything.

Interviewing the Respondent

Interviewing someone Respondent of inappropriate behavior can be a very uncomfortable situation. However, remember your job is to remain objective and to gather the facts. Gathering as much information about the claims, including physical evidence, before interviewing the Respondent allows you to remain in control of the interview, to be alert for inconsistencies, either from the Complainant or the Respondent, and prepared to ask probing questions about these inconsistencies.

Begin by explaining the general details of the complaint to the Respondent. Do not editorialize; just provide the facts as they have been relayed to you. I tend to stay away from giving complete details at the outset, but instead, outline the reason for the interview. For example, I might say, "We have received a complaint from Employee X that you have engaged in misconduct (e.g. sexual harassment, bullying, violence, theft). I want to give you an opportunity to give your side of the story and provide me with any information you have that will assist me with uncovering the facts." I give them enough information for them to wonder how much I know, to give them the opportunity to "come clean" on their own or to refute the allegations.

Please note that during the interview, you will have to disclose the complete details of the accusations. This is not a game of hide and go seek. What I explained above is merely one strategy. You can always provide all the details at the outset if you think that is a better strategy for the investigation you are conducting. Either way, carefully observe the Respondent's body language as you are providing the information. Does the person look shocked, nervous, angry, incredulous, or afraid? Advise the Respondent of any policies or laws that may be violated by the issues raised.

Ask open-ended questions. Request a chronological timeline of events from the Respondent's perspective. Keep an open mind. Do not rush to judgment. Remain impartial and be respectful. Don't allow any previous encounters you may have had with the Respondent or things you have heard to affect your questioning. Your job is to gather the facts. If the Respondent believes you have already concluded they did something wrong, you have blown your opportunity to get them to be open and honest. What you will get is a defensive and uncooperative witness.

If the Respondent does not deny the allegations, here are some questions to ask to gather the facts.

SAMPLE QUESTIONS FOR THE RESPONDENT

1. Explain to me in a narrative format, what happened.

2. When did the incident(s) occur?

3. Where did the incident(s) occur?

4. Was anyone else involved?

5. Were there any witnesses? Who and what is their position?

6. How did the Complainant react to these actions at the time?

7. What was your response to the Complainant's reaction?

8. Do you have any physical evidence (e.g., emails, text messages, social media posts, photos, video)?

9. Why did you engage in this behavior?

10. Have you engaged in this behavior with any other employees?

11. Have you discussed your behavior towards Complainant with any other employee or a member of management? To whom and when?

12. Detail any discussions you had regarding your behavior towards the Complainant.

13. Is there anyone else we should speak with concerning these allegations? Who? What would those people know?

14. Have you engaged in any other inappropriate behavior that we should know about? Please explain.

Be prepared, the Respondent may deny the allegations. Do not let that deter you. Keep asking questions.

SAMPLE QUESTIONS WHEN THE RESPONDENT DENIES THE ALLEGATIONS
1. Why do you think someone would make these claims about you?
2. Are there any witnesses who will support your version of the events?
3. Do you have any documentation or other physical evidence to contradict the claims?
4. Is there anything that you can think of that may have occurred between you and the Complainant that she may have misinterpreted as inappropriate behavior?

Notetaking During Interviews

Your documentation of the information provided by witnesses is not only important to your decision-making process but may be valuable if the employee later files a claim or lawsuit.

BEST PRACTICES FOR NOTE-TAKING

- Document the date and time of the interview.

- Identify all people present.

- Make a list of your questions or outline your areas of inquiry.

- Document specific responses, notable quotes, details, who, what, when, where, why.

- Do not use legal words/assessments/conclusions – only include facts.

- Do not include your personal opinions, judgments, off-color remarks, or inflammatory words in your notes.

- Record any significant or unusual occurrences during the interview (e.g. witness crying, yelling, refusing to answer questions, unusual body language).

Written Witness Statements

You may find that it is beneficial to have witnesses provide a written statement, particularly if your workforce is transient, e.g., the hospitality, retail, and restaurant industries. If you decide to get a written statement, make sure the statement is signed and that the employee's name is also printed legibly so his/her identity can be ascertained later. Also, if one of these witnesses leaves your organization, make sure you have forwarding contact information and their social security number. The latter will help with locating the witness if the contact information is no longer valid. Witness statements should be kept as part of the investigative file and should not be provided to the Complainant, the Respondent, or other witnesses.

Closing Out Interviews

At the end of each interview, ask close-out questions such as:

- Is there anything else you think I need to know?

- Who else should I speak with?

- What other documents may be relevant to this investigation?

- Is there any question you think I should have asked you but did not?

- Did you understand all the questions I asked you?

- Do you need to change any of your answers or have you now recalled information that you did not earlier?

Before the witness leaves, let them know that they can contact you in the future to provide any additional information. Remind the witness about producing any documents they agreed to provide and set a deadline for receipt of the documents. Finally, remind the witness that they will not be retaliated against and that if they feel that retaliation is occurring, they should immediately report that to HR or a manager.

Bottom Line

At all times, you must remain in control of the interview.

NEVER LET THEM SEE YOU SWEAT

- Ask some general introductory questions first (name, position, job duties)

- Make the witness feel comfortable. Establish rapport by asking neutral baseline questions

- Briefly explain the reason they are being interviewed and the benefits of cooperating

- Do not emphasize the disadvantages of not cooperating.

- Be courteous.

- Speak to the witness, not at or down to them.

- Ask clear, concise, open-ended questions.

- Allow the witness to speak and explain.

- Resist the urge to interrupt, but do not be afraid to focus the witness, if needed.

- Elicit as much first-hand information as you can. However, do not disregard hearsay statements as those statements may lead you to relevant information.

- Minimize asking "why" questions. If you must, try to do so towards the end of the interview. You want to know – who, what, when, where, how.

- Take a break and reconvene if necessary.

***

ACE YOUR WORKPLACE INVESTIGATION

1. Using our case study on pages 32-33, what facts do you believe are missing and need to be discovered during the investigation?

2. List 5 questions you would ask the Complainant.

3. List 5 questions you would ask the Respondent.

4. List 5 questions you would ask any of the employees, other than Complainant, who claimed the Respondent harassed them.

5. List 5 questions you would ask any of the managers.

6. Are there any other types of body language you think would assist you in assessing a witness' credibility? If so, what behavior(s) would you look for and what do you believe that behavior would tell you about the witnesses' credibility?

* * *

NOTES

NOTES

NOTES

NOTES

GATHERING PHYSICAL EVIDENCE

Documents create a paper reality we call proof.
–Mason Cooley

Testimony gathered from witnesses during interviews is just one type of evidence. You should also be gathering as much physical evidence as possible concurrently with doing the interviews or shortly after the interview is concluded.

Types of Physical Evidence

Physical evidence, such as documents, are useful for refreshing a witnesses' recollection or to evaluate motive or intent. Physical evidence may also be more reliable, as it is usually a representation of facts at the time, or close to the time when the alleged incidents occurred. That does not mean that physical evidence is always reliable. We all know that this evidence can be altered or otherwise manipulated.

As many would say, "in the old days," physical evidence was likely to be only in the form of handwritten notes or maybe some journal entries. However, in this technological age, the sources of physical evidence seem endless. The following chart includes some of the types of physical evidence you should request from witnesses during the interview. Your organization may also need to search its own email servers, calendaring systems, employee files, and managements' files to gather additional physical evidence.

TYPES OF PHYSICAL EVIDENCE
• Emails
• Calendar entries
• Text messages
• Photographs
• Videos
• Recordings
• Voicemails
• Facebook posts
• Instagram posts
• Twitter feeds
• Handwritten notes
• Journals
• WhatsApp posts
• YouTube videos
• Social Media such as LinkedIn, Instant Messenger, Pinterest

Documenting Receipt of Evidence

When you receive physical evidence from a witness, you need to maintain its integrity to counter any claims of tampering or regarding authenticity. This process is referred to as "chain of custody." A standard chain of custody form should include at least the following:

- The identity of the person providing the document

- The date you received the document

- The original source of the document, if known

- The author of the document, if known

- The identity of any recipients of the document if not ascertainable from the document.

See Illustration No. 2 for a sample "Chain of Custody" form.

ILLUSTRATION NO. 2

SAMPLE CHAIN OF CUSTODY FORM

Date of Complaint: _____

Complainant Name & Position: _____

Respondent Name & Position: _____

Complaint Intake Investigator: _____

Person providing evidence	Description	Source/ Author/ Recipients of evidence	Location	Date Received	Received By

DISPOSAL OF EVIDENCE

Reason for disposal: _____

Name of person authorizing disposal: _____

Date of authorization: _____

Method of disposal: _____

If you receive documents in an electronic format, to avoid any claims of alteration, make every effort to preserve the metadata. If you're like me when I first heard the term, you're probably saying meta who, meta what? So, let me help you out.

> Metadata describes other data. It provides information about a certain item's content. For example, an image may include metadata that describes how large the picture is, the color depth, the image resolution, when the image was created, and other data. A text document's metadata may contain information about how long the document is, who the author is, when the document was written, and a short summary of the document.[12]

Metadata is one way of authenticating documents. You can locate metadata information in the "properties" tab of documents. For further information on preserving metadata, you should contact your IT professional.

Finally, *do* not write on or alter documents in any way. If you want to take notes or annotate the document in any way, make a copy of the original and use the copy as your working document.

During the investigation, maintain any physical evidence you received in a password protected electronic file or in a locked cabinet. This information should only be shared on a need-to-know basis. Later, we will discuss what to do with this evidence once the investigation is completed.

* * *

ACE YOUR WORKPLACE INVESTIGATION

1. Using our case study on pages 32-33, what types of physical evidence would you request from witnesses?

2. During your witness interviews, you received the following physical evidence:

    a. Copies of text messages from the Respondent to Employee Y.

    b. Email messages between employees about the Respondent's behavior.

    c. Copies of journal entries made by one of the witnesses.

    d. Witness statements referenced in the Complainant's complaint.

    e. Printouts of Facebook posts by employees about the Respondent.

3. What additional information do you need about these documents to complete the chain of custody form for each of the above?

4. Assume you received that information, use Illustration No. 2 on page 114, to complete a Chain of Custody Form for each of these documents.

* * *

NOTES

NOTES

NOTES

NOTES

PART V: DECIDE

DELIBERATING

Sound and just decisions are products of deliberative thought.

–Kelly Charles-Collins

Review your investigation plan. Have you addressed all the issues raised in the complaint? Have you interviewed all the witnesses identified in the complaint, revealed during interviews, or witnesses who otherwise would reasonably be believed to have information about the claims? Have you re-interviewed any witnesses to clarify information or gather additional information? Have witnesses provided you all the documentation you have requested? Have you asked the right open-ended questions, gathered physical evidence and uncovered the facts? If you answered "Yes" to *all* these questions, it is now time to deliberate, analyze the information, and make a decision. This process is the same whether you have multiple witnesses, or you are faced with only the Complainant versus the Respondent.

Evaluate Your Findings

To make a sound decision, you must evaluate all the information you received during the investigation. As the old saying goes, there are three sides to every story. Finding the truth about a complaint requires an objective, impartial analysis of all the evidence. Context is everything. What may seem on its own not to make sense, or to corroborate or negate a complaint or denial, in context may complete the puzzle.

To deliberate means carefully considering and examining the information you received, before making an objective decision. This is not the time to guess or just go with your gut, but that doesn't mean you should abandon your common sense or instincts.

Create a timeline of events. Look for consistencies and inconsistencies. Prepare a chart to outline testimony or physical evidence that corroborates or refutes the complaints. I find that creating a visualization of the evidence aids my analysis. You should also assess the credibility of the Complainant, the Respondent and the fact witnesses. Ask yourself the following questions as you analyze each witness' statements and the physical evidence.

ASSESSING CREDIBILITY
• Is the statement believable on its face?
• Does it make sense?
• Did the witness seem to be telling the truth, lying or being evasive?
• Did the witness have a reason to lie?
• Is there a backstory?
• Is there other witness testimony or physical evidence that corroborates or contradicts the witnesses' version of events?
• Does the Respondent have a history of similar behavior or complaints?
• Did the witness have the ability (e.g., present on the date(s), time(s), location(s)) to witness the things about

which they testified?

- Were the witnesses being helpful, evasive, direct?
- What did you observe about their body language during the interviews?

Potential outcomes of the Investigation

Based on the information you received, you must make a decision, i.e., determine the outcome of your investigation. Does the testimony and physical evidence support or negate the claims? Is the evidence inconclusive? Did the evidence raise other issues in the workplace that need to be addressed? Is this a matter that needs to be escalated to upper management, ownership, the board of directors, or an attorney?

Depending on the answers to these questions, your deliberation will result in one of several outcomes. The goal of an effective investigation is to reach a concrete, objective conclusion. However, that is not always possible. Following are the possible outcomes of an investigation.

POTENTIAL INVESTIGATION OUTCOMES

- Inappropriate conduct did occur and/or organization policy, federal or state law was violated
- Inappropriate conduct did not occur and/or organization policy, federal or state law was not violated
- The investigation was inconclusive or
- Further investigation is required by outside counsel or a consultant.

* * *

Preparing the Final Report

The devil is in the details.

–Unknown

So now that you have deliberated, decided the outcome and determined the appropriate corrective action, if any, it's time to write your report. Your report may be produced later in litigation or other investigative proceedings and may be seen by outside entities such as attorneys, judges, jurors, outside counsel, auditors, or other investigators. Therefore, it is imperative that your report is detailed and accurate. It must also be objective and based on the facts derived from the witness statements and physical evidence reviewed.

Do not include your personal opinions about the evidence or witnesses, derogatory remarks or other commentaries that could be interpreted as evidence of bias. Your report must be a factual record and analysis of what you heard and what you saw – that's it. Therefore, just as Joe Friday used to say in the television show Dragnet, *"Just the facts, ma'am."* See Illustration No. 3 for a sample "Investigation Report."

Illustration No. 3

SAMPLE INVESTIGATION REPORT
(Type or write legibly)

Date: _____ Author: _____

Complainant Name & Position: _____

Respondent Name & Position: _____

SUMMARY OF COMPLAINT
(Include how complaint was initiated)

SUMMARY OF FACTS

Investigation Process: (Outline all the steps you took in conducting the investigation, including whether you informed the Complainant, and all witnesses that they are protected from retaliation for raising the complaint or participating in the investigation.)

_____

_____

Were employees told to keep investigation confidential?

____ Yes ____ No

If yes, detail all facts and circumstances that led to that decision

_____

_____

Page 1 of 3

WITNESSES				
Witness Name	Date & Location	Interviewer Name	Other People Present	Written witness statement (Y/N)

Identify any documents reviewed:

_____

_____

Conclusions: (Support with witness statements and physical evidence. Articulate basis for any credibility determinations. Specifically reference any relevant company policies.)

_____

_____

_____

Recommendation for Corrective Action:

_____

_____

_____

Name and title of Author

_____

Signature

_____

Identify each person involved in the final determination as to the corrective action taken:

Name & Title:

_____

Name & Title:

_____

What corrective action, if any, will be taken:

_____

_____

_____

_____

_____

_____

Date corrective action taken/communicated:

_____

Documentation of corrective action: _____ Yes _____ No

Name & title of person communicating corrective action:

_____

Additional comments about investigation:

_____

_____

_____

_____

BEST PRACTICES FOR REPORT WRITING

- Type the report. If you're handwriting looks like mine, the universe will thank you.

- Date the report. This seems like a "duh," but you would be surprised how many reports I have received that are not dated.

- Legibly identify the author(s) of the report or any person who contributed to or reviewed the report. Weeks, months or years from now when you are sipping Pina Coladas on the beach, the rest of us will need to know who wrote the report.

- Explain what necessitated the investigation (e.g., employee complaint, charge of discrimination, demand letter, lawsuit, direction of legal counsel).

- Identify the name of the Complainant.

- Outline the issues raised by the complaint.

- Outline all the steps you took in conducting the investigation, including whether you informed the Complainant and all witnesses that they are protected from retaliation for raising the complaint or participating in the investigation.

- Include a summary of the facts gathered during the investigation and include a chronology of events, where applicable.

- If you made an individualized determination that the investigation should be kept confidential, detail all facts and circumstances that led to making that decision.

- List the names of all witnesses interviewed, date interviewed, location and names of any witnesses present during the interview.

- Include, in quotes, any admissions of wrongdoing by the Respondent.

- List any documents reviewed and the source of each document.

- Explain any conclusions reached, supported by witness statements and documents where possible. This is not the time for short-cuts. In real estate, it's location, location, location. In investigations, it's detail, detail, detail.

- Do not make legal conclusions. This is a factual investigation.

- If your conclusions are based on weighing the credibility of witnesses, articulate why you gave more weight to one witness' testimony over another's.

- Reference any policies that relate to the conduct in question – quote the policy and note the version of the policy (e.g., date, version).

- If your investigation was inconclusive, specifically explain why you reached that conclusion.

- If you decide to take corrective action, explain your rationale for the proposed action. Ensure your decision is fair and proportionate to the misconduct and is consistent with action taken in the past for similar situations.

- Identify each person who was involved in the final determination as to the corrective action taken.

- If you decide the investigation needs to be turned over to a consultant or an attorney, explain why.

As Columbo would say, *"Just one more thing."* Remember FACTA, from page 57, well, she's back. If you use a third-party to conduct workplace investigations, you do not have to disclose the contents of the investigation prior to taking corrective action based on the report. Additionally, just as with an in-house investigation, you do not have to provide the Respondent a copy of the third-party's report. However, if you take adverse action based on the third party's report, you must disclose a summary of the third-party report to the Respondent in the investigation. The summary should only include the nature and substance of the report. You do not have to identify the witnesses interviewed or other sources of information.

* * *

ACE YOUR WORKPLACE INVESTIGATIONS

1. Using our case study (pages 32-33) and the sample Investigation Report Form, Illustration No. 3 (pages 126-128), complete the summary section of the report.

2. Go back to your response to question number 5 on page 84, regarding confidentiality and complete that section of the report.

3. Assume that during the investigation you discovered the following facts:

   a. The Respondent grabbed Employee Y's butt on one occasion two years prior to Complainant's report to HR,

   b. The Respondent asked Employee Z out for dinner and drinks several times in the year prior to Complainant's report, despite Employee Z repeatedly denying his requests,

c. The Respondent did not rub against Employee X's breast,

d. Manager C brushed off Complainant's reports of the Respondent's inappropriate behavior and did not report the claims to HR,

e. The Respondent's comments that Complainant's job performance was poor were accurate.

4. What corrective action would you take against the Respondent and why?

5. Would you take corrective action against any other employees?

6. Using the physical evidence listed on page 116, complete the documents reviewed section of the report.

* * *

NOTES

NOTES

NOTES

NOTES

TAKING
CORRECTIVE ACTION

It's not how we make mistakes, but how we correct them that defines us.

—Rachel Wolchin

You have concluded the investigation. Now you must determine what, if any, corrective action will be taken and against whom. You should consider the following:

- If you are unable to reach a determination or believe that the investigation requires input from legal counsel or an outside consultant, you should notify the appropriate organization representative.

- If inappropriate conduct **did not** occur and/or organization policy, federal or state law was not violated, or the investigation was inconclusive, you should still follow up with training to reinforce the organization's policies and procedures.

- If inappropriate conduct **did** occur and/or an organization policy, federal or state law was violated, *you must take immediate, appropriate corrective action.*

Remember, you may need to take corrective action against more than one employee. Caution – that other employee should rarely if ever, be the Complainant. If you find yourself itching to take corrective action against the complainant, contact your employment lawyer first.

You must take corrective measures to rectify the inappropriate conduct or put safeguards in place to ensure that the type of behavior complained of, stops and does not occur in the future. To determine the appropriate action to take, some things to consider are the severity and frequency of the misconduct, prior incidents by the Respondent, the likelihood that corrective action less than termination will rectify the Respondent's behavior, and how similar incidents by other employees have been treated in the past.

If there is no similar prior incident, evaluate whether the corrective action you are recommending is something you feel comfortable with, as it will be setting a precedent for future incidents.

EXAMPLES OF CORRECTIVE ACTION

- Appropriate discipline (e.g. suspension) of the Respondent or other employees who have also engaged in misconduct (consider the conduct, consider past practice, work rules, employee handbook, etc.)

- Mediation between the employees

- Termination of Respondent or other employees who were found to also have engaged in misconduct

- Reporting criminal conduct to law enforcement

- Training of staff regarding company policies and employment laws

- Updating or changing organization policies

If you are not terminating an employee, your goal with corrective action should be to not only rectify but to change and deter the inappropriate behavior. Therefore, corrective action should be proportionate to the offense. Remember, you must be consistent or risk a potential discrimination claim.

After you determine what appropriate corrective action should be taken, you must document your decision. You should include your decision in your final report, which is a company document not to be shared with employees. Thus, you must also document the corrective action on a separate written form that must be placed in the employee's personnel file after communication with the employee. See Illustration No. 4 for a sample "Corrective Action Form."

Do not place a copy of this corrective action documentation in the Complainant's or any witnesses' personnel file.

* * *

ACE YOUR WORKPLACE INVESTIGATIONS

1. Based on the type of disciplinary action you decided to take against the Respondent in our case study, complete your sample Corrective Action Form.

Illustration No. 4

SAMPLE CORRECTIVE ACTION FORM

Name: _____   Date: _____

Reason for Disciplinary Action:

___ Policy violation   ____ Insubordination   ____ Conduct

___ Absenteeism   ____ Job Performance   ____ Safety

___ Other

Description of Incident(s) (include specific policy violated):

_____

_____

Action Taken:

___ Coaching   ___ Verbal Counseling   ___ Written Warning

___ Suspension   ____ Termination   ____ Other _____

Employee Comments:

_____

_____

This disciplinary action is a formal warning. Failure to improve this behavior and/or further violation of company policy or other inappropriate conduct, will result in further disciplinary action up to and including discharge. By signing below, you acknowledge that you have received this notice.

Employee: _____   Date: _____

Company Representative:

_____

(Print name)

Company Representative: _____(Signature)

Title: _____   Date: _____

NOTES

NOTES

NOTES

NOTES

NOTES

Retaining and Disposing Evidence

Finally, it's okay to be a hoarder — at least for a while.

Unknown

Once the investigation is complete, the initial complaint, witness statements, documents, final report, and any documentation or record of corrective action taken should be maintained in a secure investigation file identified by Complainant's name. This file should only be accessible to people with a need to know this information.

Do not put this information in the Complainant's or witness' personnel files. If corrective action is taken against the Respondent, documentation of that action is the only thing that should be placed in their personnel file.

Many organizations have document retention/destruction policies which provide for the disposal of documents at various planned intervals. Additionally, there are laws relating to retention of specific types of documents (e.g., payroll, I-9 forms, personnel files, job applications, drug test results). Therefore, b*efore you dispose of any physical evidence or information gathered during an investigation, consult with an experienced employment attorney.* Disposing of evidence that is relevant to a pending claim or lawsuit could subject the organization to sanctions and/or other adverse rulings based on claims of "spoliation" of evidence. Spoliation is the intentional, reckless, or negligent withholding, hiding, altering, fabricating, or destroying of evidence relevant to a legal proceeding.[13]

* * *

PART VI: COMMUNICATE THE DECISION

COMMUNICATING
YOUR DECISION

*Leadership is a way of thinking, a way of acting
and, most importantly, a way of communicating.*
                                        –Simon Sinek

Whatever your decision, both the Complainant and the Respondent must be notified that the investigation has been concluded. These notifications should be done in person, when possible. When meeting with the Complainant or Respondent, you should provide a verbal summary overview of your investigation. Avoid providing specific information or testimony received from witnesses to avoid any potential friction between the employees.

Inform the Complainant of the outcome of the investigation — whether it was substantiated, not substantiated, inconclusive, or requires further investigation by an outside investigator. If you decided to take corrective action, you should verbally advise the Complainant that appropriate corrective action will be taken, but you should not provide details of the specific action(s) to be taken.

You must advise the Respondent of any corrective action which will be taken. Explain what policy or law you believe was violated based on your investigation of the claims. This information should be included on the Corrective Action Form, which should be provided to the Respondent for review. Allow the Respondent to write any comments on the form. If the Respondent raises new claims, you will need to investigate those claims. If the claims are truly new claims and not a rehash of old claims by the Respondent and they are related to the current investigation, you must re-open your investigation before taking any further action. If the claims are new, unrelated claims, you must begin a new investigation.

Remember that employees are never *required* to sign the Corrective Action Form. But, if they refuse to sign the form, simply notate that they refused. If the claim involved sexual harassment, discrimination or retaliation provide a copy of the organization's respective policy to the Respondent. Have the Respondent review the policy, sign, and date the policy. Place the original in the Respondent's personnel file and give a copy to the Respondent. If the claim was a violation of any other policy, review that policy with the Respondent and ensure that you have an updated signed handbook acknowledgement on file.

If you determined that employees other than the Respondent should be disciplined, follow the same process as with the Respondent. Additionally, if you determine that the violation involved criminal conduct, you may need to notify the appropriate authorities. However, in those circumstances, unless there is an urgent need such as impending violence, best practice is to consult with legal counsel before making any such notification.

Whether the Respondent or another employee, if you decide to terminate an employee, keep your communications simple and broad. You do not want to be pigeon-holed to a specific reason, which later may be challenged due to inconsistent application. Instead, leave yourself wiggle room, truthful wiggle room, and only say they are being terminated for "job performance," "insubordination," "violation of company policies," of some other general category of misconduct.

* * *

Finally, no matter what, **train all employees.** A little training never hurt anybody. It could be a formal training, or if there was recent formal training, you could do a review of policies during team meetings or morning roll call. You have heard the phrase, "Where there's smoke, there's fire." The complaint you investigated may not have proven true, but the fact there was a complaint is a red flag that there may be other issues brewing. So, even if you decide no violation occurred or the evidence was inconclusive, it is a good idea to conduct or make a recommendation for training after you complete your investigation.

This will show the organization's commitment to enforcing policies and ensuring that those policies are communicated to employees. It will also show employees that their voices are being heard.

* * *

ACE YOUR WORKPLACE INVESTIGATION

1. Assume that you have decided there is no evidence to support the Complainant's and the other employees' claims about the Respondent.

   a. How would you communicate your findings to the Complainant?

   b. How would you communicate your findings to the Respondent?

2. Assume that you have decided there is evidence to support the Complainant's and the other employees'

claims about the Respondent and you have decided to terminate the Respondent.

a. How would you communicate your findings to the Complainant?

b. How would you communicate your decision to terminate to the Respondent?

* * *

NOTES

NOTES

NOTES

NOTES

PART VII: CULTIVATE

EARNING TRUST

People will forget what you said … forget what you did, but people will never forget the way you made them feel.

–Maya Angelou

You can do it! You will accept my recommendation to always conduct an investigation. But don't get too excited. Depending on the outcome of your investigation, this may be the only praise you get.

Don't expect a pat on your back. This is your job. If your findings support the Complainant's claims, the Complainant may or may not feel vindicated because they may not know what specific corrective action has or will be taken. If your findings are inconclusive or do not support the Complainant's claims, buckle up! Be prepared for the backlash and the claims of, "I told you nothing was going to happen, "You only care about protecting the organization." Your instinct may be to react and explain all the ways you were objective and try to convince the Complainant that you were not just protecting the organization. Resist the urge. If you are itching to respond, remember this:

"Anything you say, can and will be held against you."

Instead, actively listen to any concerns and assure the Complainant that their complaint was taken seriously, a thorough investigation was conducted, and any necessary, appropriate corrective action was taken. You should also encourage the employee to follow-up with you, a supervisor, Human Resources, or other management if any other issues arise. Likewise, you should follow-up with the Complainant in about two weeks to ensure there are no other issues.

You will never please everyone. However, consistently following the steps in this book and asking the right questions will assist you in meeting your goals of uncovering facts, identifying areas of opportunity, reducing the necessity for employee complaints, minimizing legal risk to the organization, all while earning employee trust by being professional, thorough, fair and consistent.

* * *

Ace Your Workplace Investigations

Avoid Friction, Cover Your Assets, and Earn Employee Trust

Reaping the Benefits

Knowledge is of no value unless you put it into practice.

–Anton Chekhov

To reap the benefits of your hard work, you need to cultivate good habits. Below are some principles that will guide you on your way.

GUIDING PRINCIPLES
• Be professional, fair, consistent, respectful and objective.
• Implement company policy that outlines the protocol for workplace investigations.
• Ensure that the investigation is conducted by a thorough, trained, impartial, discrete and yes, nosey investigator.
• Develop some core open-ended interview questions.
• Implement procedures to ensure the investigation is conducted promptly after an employee complaint.
• Do not lose control or compromise the process.
• Know when to outsource the investigation to an attorney or third-party consultant.
• Make sure the investigation is thorough and free

from the influence of persons whom the employee may claim had a bias against them and thus tainted the investigation.

- Do not guarantee confidentiality.

- When developing your investigation strategy, if you determine confidentiality is required, set forth in writing the specific factors justifying the legitimate business justification for confidentiality. Maintain this document in the investigation file.

- If a gag order is necessary, narrowly tailor it to achieve the legitimate business justification. Additionally, limit the timeframe to the pendency of the investigation.

- If you cannot justify a gag order, take reasonably necessary precautions to ensure the integrity of the investigation. Proper planning, e.g., determining the order of witness interviews, will help to achieve this goal.

- Revise or rescind any existing confidentiality policy regarding internal investigations, so that it does not impose a blanket rule, but rather explains to employees that confidentiality may be requested on a case-by-case basis where necessary to achieve legitimate business needs.

- Revise or rescind any policies that could be interpreted to prohibit employees for complaining about the terms and conditions of employment with co-workers or third parties.

- If the company policy includes a disciplinary clause for breach of the confidentiality policy, revise any mandatory language to be discretionary so as not to run afoul of the EEOC's position regarding retaliation.

- Communicate your decision to all necessary parties, but only provide specifics to upper management, the board of directors, the owners, or your attorneys. Do not provide specifics to the Complainant or any other employee.

- Take prompt corrective action.

- Follow-up with the Complainant.

- Disseminate the organization's policies and any updates to policies, to employees.

- Continuously train employees and management. Document the training, including topics discussed. Maintain employee sign-in sheets or other record of attendance.

* * *

HR Jingle

Based on Aretha Franklin's song, Respect.

A little jingle I wrote to remind you how to gain the trust of your employees, but most of all to make you smile.

T-R-U-S-T

Find out what it means to me

T-R-U-S-T

Take care, CCC

Oh (communicate, collaborate, cultivate)

A little TRUST

T, T, T

T, T, T, Trust

* * *

ABOUT THE AUTHOR:
KELLY CHARLES-COLLINS

Kelly Charles-Collins has been successfully defending small businesses to Fortune 100 corporations against employee lawsuits since 1998. She aids her clients by providing them with day-to-day preventive counseling, developing company policies, training management and employees, assessing and implementing workplace solutions, and conducting workplace investigations. As a trial attorney, Kelly understands the tangible and intangible impact of deficient, non-existent, or inconsistent application of processes and policies on the workplace and its employees.

But she's not just an attorney. Kelly is a skilled public speaker, author, arbitrator, and Human Resources expert. She has worked for Publix Super Markets, Inc., a Fortune 100 corporation, where she conducted workplace investigations; she's a former business owner; and she founded and led a non-profit for breast cancer awareness. These experiences enable her to understand the personal motivators and internal business factors that drive decision-makers.

Kelly believes that HR, at its best, is an interactive, collaborative process between management and employees driven by open communication, shared goals, and mutual benefit. She boils it down to her "3 C's – Communicate, Collaborate, Cultivate."SM With her proactive approach to human resources risk management, Kelly works with organizations to develop healthy, inclusive, respectful, environments that deliver results. Conducting effective workplace investigations is an essential part of that process.

An in-demand speaker, Kelly has presented at the HR Star Conference in Atlanta since 2015; lectured and presented a three-part webinar series for the University of Miami and Continuing Legal Education webinars for LawPractice CLE; been invited to speak for the Discovery Recruiters Network; and spoken at the Claims and Litigation Retail, Restaurant, and Hospitality Conference; the National Minority and Women-Owned Law Firms Annual Conference; St. Leo University in Tampa; the Greater Tampa Chamber of Commerce; The Seminar Group's 8th Annual Labor & Employment Law Conference; Trial Advocacy Bootcamp; and many others. She also had a featured article in the Tampa Bay Parenting Magazine, was featured in The Tampa Bay Business *Journal* and appeared on internet radio on *That Business Show.*

* * *

REASONS TO HIRE
KELLY CHARLES-COLLINS

Hiring the right speaker, like hiring an attorney, is a very important decision.

Kelly makes that decision easy for you. Your attendees will be interacting and engaging with someone who has successfully worked with small businesses to Fortune 500 and 100 companies to develop healthy, inclusive, respectful, environments that deliver results.

With her breadth and depth of knowledge of Human Resources and Employment Law, Kelly delivers customized keynotes, training, and consulting tailored to align with your business objectives.

Here are a few reasons why meeting planners, associations, and corporations love working with Kelly:

1. *Kelly is real, relatable, and realistic*

Kelly is as real as it gets – a true "salt of the earth." Not afraid to share her own challenges and triumphs, Kelly will give you the good, the bad, and the ugly. However, she also provides realistic, practical advice to help your organization overcome challenges. Kelly enjoys meeting and speaking with her audiences and makes herself available to add value for your attendees. Your attendees will always leave Kelly's presentations feeling enlightened and empowered and with practical tips they can implement immediately.

2. *You are the star*

Kelly is client-focused. She ensures that you, your client and your attendees are the focus. Kelly's mission is to be the light for others — revealing their passion, purpose, and greatness. She believes in legacy building. Kelly develops customized keynotes, training, and consultations that align with your business or personal principles and objectives.

3. *Credibility and Integrity*

Kelly knows her stuff. She has guided hundreds of organizations – from small businesses to Fortune 500 companies – to discover the hidden truths about their workplace. An employment attorney with more than 20 years of experience, she conducts workplace investigations and provides training and coaching programs to help companies reduce bias, eliminate harassment, and banish incivility. With her expert guidance, Kelly guides organizations to nurture trust and respect so they can create diverse, inclusive, and harmonious cultures.

4. *Strategic Partner*

Kelly is here for you. She will work with you to make sure the event goes off without a hitch. Need marketing support? You can count of Kelly's support. If there is a hitch, you never have to worry that Kelly will switch to Diva mode. When you work with Kelly, it is a partnership. Kelly will work hard to accommodate your requests, whenever possible, attend receptions, networking events, and/or other pre- or post-events with your sponsors, attendees, and clients.

5. *She's Exciting and Engaging*

There is nothing boring about a Kelly presentation. They are interactive and thought provoking. Kelly connects with her audiences and brings them in to her presentation with her visual presentations and her stories. Don't be surprised - sometimes there's even music and dancing.

6. *Audiences Love Her*

Kelly consistently receives near perfect ratings from attendees at the presentations. Once you hear Kelly speak, you will understand why. A left brain/right brain lawyer, Kelly is an analytical free-spirit, which draws the different personalities in your audience to her. You, your client, and your attendees will leave wanting more.

7. *No Legal-Ease*

Kelly is an experienced and skilled attorney, but you never have to worry that your audiences won't understand her. She does not speak in "legal-ease." Kelly is adept at delivering complex legal and HR issues in an understandable practical way.

* * *

Next Action Steps

GO TO
WWW.KELLYCHARLESCOLLINS.COM

- Not sure if you answered the questions correctly?
- Have questions about the contents of the book?
- Ready to ACE Your Workplace Investigations?
- Need training for your organization?

Work directly with Kelly:

1. *Keynotes*
2. *Breakout Sessions*
3. *HR Consulting*
4. *Interactive Masterclasses*
5. *One-to-One or Group Coaching*

Connect with Kelly!

Website: www.KellyCharlesCollins.com
Email: kelly@kellycharlescollins.com
Twitter: @hrlawattorney
Instagram: kellycharlescollins
LinkedIn: www.linkedin.com/in/kellycharlescollins
Facebook: www.Facebook.com/kellycharlescollins22

Acknowledgements

To the many people who have attended my seminars on how to conduct effective workplace investigations and provided such positive and insightful feedback — thank you.

I would also thank some very specific people:

Tears came to my eyes as I thought about how to thank my mom, Sonia Charles. I have no bigger cheerleader in life than my mom. As a little girl, because I wouldn't leave her side, my family nicknamed me my mother's "deodorant." She taught me about strength of character and integrity; love and respect; self-confidence and grace; courage and perseverance. Because of her, I grew up believing I could be and do anything. She celebrates my every accomplishment, no matter how small. She *is* the wind beneath my wings.

My dad, Beverley "Teddy" Charles, the person with whom I have the great pleasure of sharing a birthday. He was instrumental in reviewing early versions of this book and providing very meaningful feedback. He is the epitome of the phrase "still waters run deep." In his quiet way, he has always held me up and rooted me on. I am a Daddy's girl.

What can I say about my sister, Lisa-Rene Charles. I could not ask for a better sister. She has been a sounding board, a lightning rod, my dance partner with Les Twins, and my Jamaican banana chips sharer. When I was a little girl, hating anything named school, I hid under her desk with my little dirty pillow. She has always been my comfort and my shelter.

My dear husband, John Collins, who endures my late nights in front of the computer and my every crazy whim. He may not always understand it all or agree, but he has my back no matter what. Like my dad, in his quiet way, he encourages me. He's a special kind of southern gentleman and I am blessed he is my hubby.

Words are not enough to thank my son, Jordan Charles a/k/a DJ Don Chido, who since birth has given me someone to fight for, someone to live for, someone to excel for, someone to be great for, just someone to be whatever I dream of being. You are my light and my mirror. As we say in Jamaica, I love you more than cooked food.

My niece, Danielle Hercules, I see myself in you — your strength of character, your drive, your creativity, your fashion sense, your no-nonsense attitude. Keep striving for greatness.

My aunt and godmother, Patricia Edwards — I know you think we don't listen to you when you speak, but we do; I do. When I moved to Tampa, you told me to live big. Well Goddy, here we go!

My late aunt, Kay Anderson, who implored me to love myself more than I loved anyone else, so I *could* love anyone else. Titty Kay, as I affectionately called her, was an award-winning artist and author. I know she is so proud of me and this book.

My aunt Elaine Hamilton, my second mother. Ever since I was a little girl, you have been there for me. Your joy in my success sustains me.

Thank you to my Irie Family, my cousins, David Anderson, Karen Anderson, Gordon Edwards, Dory

Edwards. One love. The daily laughs and banter on WhatsApp keep me going.

George F. Knox, "Mr. Knox," thank you for being my sponsor and helping me land my first job as an attorney and being such a dear friend to my mom and our family.

Thank you to my teachers at Vaz Preparatory School in Jamaica, West Indies, particularly Angela Feanny. I hated school, but I would not be where I am today without the educational foundation provided to me at Vaz Prep.

My coach and friend Libby Gill, thank you for your encouragement and guidance. You are amazing at helping me distill my many ideas and turn my visions into reality.

I am thankful that I was listening to the radio one day and heard someone discussing the poem "The Dash" by Linda Ellis. That poem guides the way I live my life.

Many thanks to all my friends, family, and colleagues who have always encouraged me and afforded me opportunities to soar.

My National Speakers Association Central Florida Academy (NSA-CF) mentor, Jennifer Samuel-Chance, thank you for opening my eyes to what is possible just from writing this book and for keeping me on track to get it done.

I want to acknowledge my colleagues in the National Speakers Association, especially those in my Speakers Academy for all the encouragement, inspiration, and support.

My Academy Associate Dean, Claudia Smith Virga, thank you for introducing me to my editor, Nancy L. Butler-Ross. Nancy, our first conversation was so illuminating. Because of you this book evolved into even more than I ever imagined. As I told you after our first call, you don't know what you have started. *This is only the beginning.*

Resources

* * *

ENDNOTES

[1] Simon Sinek (2014). *"Leaders Eat Last: Why Some Teams Pull Together and Others Don't,"* p.86, Penguin

[2] (English Oxford Living Dictionaries n.d.)

[3] https://www.eeoc.gov/eeoc/newsroom/release/1-25-18.cfm

[4] https://www.eeoc.gov/field/

[5] https://www.hiscox.com/documents/2017-Hiscox-Guide-to-Employee-Lawsuits.pdf

[6] https://www.fastcompany.com/40440310/employees-win-very-few-civil-rights-lawsuits

[7] https://www.justia.com/50-state-surveys/recording-phone-calls-and-conversations/

[8] *Banner Health Systems*, 362 NLRB No. 137 (June 26, 2015)

[9] https://www.nlrb.gov/rights-we-protect/whats-law/employers/interfering-employee-rights-section-7-8a1

[10] www.eeoc.gov/policy

[11] (Unknown n.d.) http://www.reid.com/pdfs/peacearticle.pdf; Essays, UK. (November 2013). The Techniques of Police Interviewing Criminology Essay. Retrieved from https://www.ukessays.com?vref=1; https://onlinelibrary.wiley.com/doi/full/10.1348/135532509X449361 (Professor Saul M. Kassin 2011)

[12] https://techterms.com/definition/metadata

[13] https://en.wikipedia.org/wiki/Spoliation_of_evidence

Made in the USA
Las Vegas, NV
06 November 2021

33836048R00105